The Tragic Comedians

JAMES HALL

The Tragic Comedians

SEVEN
MODERN BRITISH NOVELISTS

Bloomington
INDIANA UNIVERSITY PRESS

823.9109
H14t

THIS BOOK HAS BEEN PUBLISHED WITH THE ASSISTANCE
OF A GRANT FROM THE FORD FOUNDATION

47632
Aug. 1964

Second Printing

Copyright © 1963 by Indiana University Press
Manufactured in the United States of America
Library of Congress catalog card number: 63-9715

Preface

"NEVER APOLOGIZE, never explain," the title of an Edmund Wilson essay, is also a good motto for anyone who attempts criticism. Yet every writer probably has in the back of his mind an ideal preface sure to engage readers who might like his kind of book and warn off those who would like some other kind. Actually faced with this rhetorical assignment, though, he may try merely to describe.

In this case, even naming, much less describing, the subject becomes difficult. If sharp distinctions in genre ever existed outside critics' *schemata*, they do not in contemporary literature. The phrase "comic novel" occurs over and over in this book, but many of the novels have little of the lightheartedness which the words will call up for many readers. And when another word—"painful" or "tragic" or whatever—is added to suggest the dissonant and threatening in the works, the possible misunderstanding over naming increases. About the best to be said is that this book deals with novelists who make considerable use of what everyone can agree is comedy, but who so mix this with severer conflicts that the mixture becomes more important than either ingredient. Certainly I should not like to quarrel over nomenclature with any reader who agrees that the novelists treated here have something fundamental in common.

The seven writers who get a chapter each seem to me the best such novelists of the period. If there were an eighth, it would be Ivy Compton-Burnett, and if a ninth, P. H. Newby. Miss Compton-Burnett in particular commands the kind of intensity among her admirers which suggests that her work will stay alive, but she is repetitious enough in theme and tone to rank a little below the novelists discussed. Newby is thinner, and his dramatic conflicts cut less deeply, but both have comic talents which, in an age less loaded with these, would be outstanding. Not everyone of sensitivity, intelligence, and good will can be expected to agree with these choices, but, however little open evaluation appears, the novelists treated are my guesses about the best.

Since dealing with the total work of seven writers could mean only a series of glances, the book tries to take each at the top of his bent—three or four novels at most, sometimes only two. It tries to see over-all direction through the progress of main dramatic conflicts and, to a lesser degree, through tone. (Since much has been written about Joyce, he appears here only incidentally, but is assumed throughout as the explorer of many later interests.) One chapter to each writer will scarcely exhaust the possibilities of interpretation, but my aim has been to write something that may lead the general reader to the novels themselves and provide the specialist with another view of his material. The sections on development within the tradition derive more or less empirically from the individual studies.

The problem of evidence in writing about novels is a perennial one. As Albert Guerard, Jr., said some years ago, no reader can be expected to have just finished thirty or more books which the critic has chosen to write about. The effort here has been to interweave enough detail about the action to let the reader judge for himself somewhat, at least, about how convincing the ideas are.

Two of these "comic novelists," Huxley and Waugh, have made their widest reputations as satirists. A distinction seems possible—comic novels find garlic and sapphires in the mud, satiric ones find mostly garlic and blame it for not being sapphire, or comic novels are more forgiving and cheerful than satiric ones—but again the distinctions slide and there may be some gain in relating *Brave New World* and *The Loved One* to their authors' more obviously comic novels.

Though no other book has treated the modern comic tradition as such, the criticism on individual writers ranges from a good deal on Forster to almost none on L. P. Hartley. Rose Macaulay's 1938 book on Forster is largely appreciation. Lionel Trilling's, published in the early forties, gives an excellent liberal and sociological interpretation. James McConkey's more recent volume uses Forster's own theories effectively to show a tension between the voice and the themes, the mysterious and the reasonable. Not too surprisingly, a number of well-known critics have written briefer critiques—E. K. Brown, Cyril Connolly, Bonamy Dobrée, F. R. Leavis, I. A. Richards, Rex Warner, Austin Warren, and Morton Dauwen Zabel. John Harvey and Glen O. Allen have written two of the best newer articles.

Huxley and Waugh have attracted much less good criticism. John Atkins' *Aldous Huxley* concentrates on the ideas and, by going through the works evenly, emphasizes the development toward mysticism and pacificism. Alexander Henderson's 1935 book also concentrates on the ideas and takes Huxley largely on his own terms. Among the shorter studies, David Daiches' chapter in *The Novel and the Modern World* remains one of the best; Sean O'Faolain's discussion in *The Vanishing Hero* is penetrating and individual; and Jocelyn Brooke's British Council pamphlet is, like others in that series, a good brief review. Colin Wilson has joined D. S. Savage in attacking Huxley, but the best recent pieces are A. E. Dyson's on "the two nothings," Martin Kessler's on the politics, and Frederick Hoffman's on the novel of ideas.

The books on Waugh have also shown a specialized interest. Frederick J. Stopp gives some biography and treats the earlier comic novels as preludes to the more clearly Catholic writings. The title of A. A. De Vitis' short book—*Roman Holiday, The Catholic Novels of Evelyn Waugh*—indicates its direction. The articles and chapters, though, suggest an increasing range— O'Faolain and Dyson on Waugh's hero, Steven Marcus on the "art of entertainment," and Donat O'Donnell on imaginative patterns.

Among the more recent reputations, Cary has attracted the most articles and Green the most books. In fact, by the criterion of critical books, Green begins to look like a major novelist. Three have appeared, all within the past five years. Kingsley Weatherhead's *A Reading of Henry Green* shows with tact and sensitivity the importance of growth as a moral and dramatic touchstone. John Russell's perceptive and well-written book contains many detailed interpretations. Edward Stokes, whose volume appeared first, makes good use of the article criticism and provides a careful technical study. Giorgio Melchiori and Philip

Toynbee, in briefer scope, have explained Green's innovations, and Walter Allen wrote two influential earlier articles. Among the best of the close studies which have begun to appear in the magazines are those by Thomas Churchill, Barbara Davidson, and Earle Labor.

Andrew Wright's *Joyce Cary: A Preface to His Novels* remains the only full-length criticism. Walter Allen's British Book News supplement is characteristically intelligent. Hazard Adams, Charles G. Hoffman, John Holloway, Pamela Hansford Johnson, and George Woodcock have written some of the most interesting articles, and Orville Prescott and Frederick R. Karl have made the most widely noticed attacks.

No one has written a book on Powell or Hartley. Melchiori's discussion of Hartley and the American tradition and Harvey Curtis Webster's survey of his development indicate some interest. Arthur Mizener describes well the social scene in *The Music of Time,* and James Vinson and Richard J. Voorhees have helped gain some American recognition for Powell.

Real indebtedness can never be indicated by listing in a preface, but I feel special gratitude to several friends and colleagues —David Daiches, David C. Fowler, Albert C. Hamilton, Robert B. Heilman, Dr. Roger C. Hendricks, and Arnold Stein. I am also grateful to many students who have taken my seminars in recent years and have not only made valuable points but often forced me to recognize what my theory of the moment omitted. And my wife, who has a literary career of her own and does not need reflected glory, has provided the kind of insight that goes far beyond encouraging and listening.

Miss Betsy McBride gave valuable assistance with the bibliography on Cary, and Mrs. Dorothy Bowie, Mrs. Madeleine Jester, and Miss Dorothy Smiley gave important help on a manuscript often far from clear.

Finally, I am grateful to the editors of *ELH, Essays in Criticism,* and the *Kenyon Review* for permission to reprint sections which first appeared in their magazines.

JAMES HALL

August, 1962

Contents

Acknowledgments

Quotations from E. M. Forster's *Howard's End* (1910) are used by permission of Alfred A. Knopf, Inc., and Edward Arnold, Ltd.; from Aldous Huxley's *Antic Hay* (1923) by permission of Harper & Row and Chatto and Windus; from Evelyn Waugh's *The Loved One* (copyright 1948), *A Handful of Dust* (copyright 1934, © 1962), and *Vile Bodies* (copyright 1930, © 1958) by permission of Little, Brown and Company and A. D. Peters; from Henry Green's *Loving* (1945) by permission of the Viking Press and The Hogarth Press; from Joyce Cary's *The Horse's Mouth* (1944) by permission of Harper & Row and Michael Joseph; from L. P. Hartley's *My Fellow Devils* (1951) by permission of Hamish Hamilton, Ltd.; from L. P. Hartley's *The Boat* (1950) by permission of Hamish Hamilton, Ltd., and Doubleday and Company, Inc.; from Anthony Powell's *A Buyer's Market* (1952) and *The Acceptance World* (1955) (both included in *A Dance to the Music of Time,* copyright 1955 by Anthony Powell) by permission of Little, Brown and Company and William Heinemann, Ltd.

The Tragic Comedians

CHAPTER ONE

Some Premises

M Y CHIEF SURPRISE in writing this book is that no one has written it before. This could be an estimate by silence, but I suspect it is more a symptom of modern embarrassment in writing about comedy. Comedy still seems only comedy and, besides, there is a sad discrepancy of tone between it and criticism. The writer is witty, personal, symbolic, specific. The critic looking for directions is necessarily more abstract, often impersonal, seldom witty. He may find himself trying to explain the *how* of comedy in general. At best, if he admits the limitations of his medium, he can say a little about the *how* and a little more about the *where* of comedy in some novels.

Whatever the critic's difficulties, this slightly suspect mode has dominated the British novel of the past twenty-five years. Henry Green, Anthony Powell, Joyce Cary, L. P. Hartley, Ivy Compton-Burnett, P. H. Newby, and younger writers like Kingsley Amis, John Wain, and John Braine have shown a consistent quality lacking in any other form. Add Joyce, Huxley, and Waugh to the list, and the question arises whether comedy has not been the dominant mode of British fiction since the first World War. Subtract the fifty years from 1870 to 1920, and the whole of British fiction begins to look primarily—but that is not the point at issue here.

The recent success has been more than an accidental appearance of similar talents. The comic novelists have capitalized brilliantly on a tradition to meet a new literary predicament. Since only another book could demonstrate my view of how this situation has developed, it appears here as simply a series of premises.

The now legendary revolution at the turn of the century merely accelerated an existing one, which, especially on the continent, concentrated on a radical criticism of the bourgeois moral and religious order. Its subject was natural man in a mechanizing society and its weapons were shocks achieved by new means for exploring the "natural." (These techniques came primarily from anthropology, psychology, sociology, and the physical sciences.) Lionel Trilling's "On the Modern Element in Modern Literature?"* summarizes the results—a cultivation of intensity and terror, followed by a dream of leaving the society altogether.

But Trilling's essay might better have been called "What is First Generation about the First Generation?" His examples are from that period and are mostly European. By 1940, however, the radical criticism had temporarily, at least, exhausted its purpose by proving its case. "The dream of reason breeds monsters," Leslie Fiedler has said**—and, he might have added, the dream of unreason breeds new dreams of equilibrium. Human nature, too, abhors a vacuum. Actually, many of the first-generation novelists were operating on letters of credit from a fairly stable society. They were men of sensibility able to attack it recklessly because they believed that their fathers and their middle class would always be there to rebel against. When this authority disappeared, largely by agreeing about a prevailing inner terror, the literary and human problem became one of improvising conciliations "for the time being." The second war helped to make "things are tough all over" a more relevant slogan than "God is dead." The last twenty or thirty years have been a mixed period, with the conservatives writing about the old fight and explorers writing about tension between the inner rebellion and a society that they both want to join and want to leave. (Even Faulkner, whose famous novels show the absurd world, turns in his later ones toward the idea of responsibility.) In England, where comedy seems reasonable, the comic novelists have had the best medium for representing this mixed sense of reality.

The contrast with France dramatizes the British situation.

* Lionel Trilling, "On the Modern Element in Modern Literature?" *Partisan Review*, XXVIII (January, 1961).
** *Love and Death in the American Novel* (New York: 1960).

Existentialist moods in much contemporary literature suggest an "influence" greater than the philosophy itself has had. In literature existentialism is a name for a consensus to which many have contributed, but Sartre, a writer *and* a professional philosopher, has been an important broker. His diagnosis, with its threats of anguish, nothingness, and indecisiveness, has been long in the making, and the cure of commitment in good faith has its salvationist side. (European experience in this century has been so unstable that anything less shrill in either diagnosis or treatment would not gain a hearing.) Sartre's finding solid ground in subjectivity is the logic of early modern literature, though it at once raises the popular question about what prevents anyone from deciding in good faith to become a mass murderer. Sartre doubtless carries over some unasserted faith in rationality, but he sees that the clear and present dangers—for the reading public, at least—are not overenthusiastic actions, but dismay, apathy, and indecision.

This shrill dialogue of the continent is what we often think of as contemporary literature. But, since the War of the Roses, the British have had the actual experience of absorbing threats and directing orderly change. The British comic tradition is one expression of a confidence that horrors can be handled. The British may have been merely lucky, but, as every sports fan knows, the habit of winning helps win the close ones. The importance of their contemporary comedy is its ability to absorb with some cheer the shocks that elsewhere have produced a sophisticated hell-fire-and-salvation brand of existentialism. (The Absurd is, after all, a comic idea.) The British novelists knew about the absurd before it became a philosophical term, they worked in a tradition with its own kind of cheer, and they realized that cheer, to earn its way, had to engage the worst that could be said about pain. In recent years they have spoken for a precarious sanity that can face horrors and retain some self-command; they speak for the human element which does not quite accept the logic of the terrors it has proved.

I do not want to argue too heavily the seriousness of comedy, since nothing is easier than to burlesque its kind of seriousness. Still, the suspicion has been about for a long time that, to have any bite, it must arise from issues that people care about. Yet this recognition goes against the grain; anyone who has lectured to audiences where the question of genre comes up knows the hope for purity. Tragic issues should evolve into pure tragedy, whatever that is, rather than the mixture they become in Faulkner or Conrad. Comedy should stick to its last.

In spite of their present dominance, the recent novelists may all be minor. As such guesses go, I would register them on posterity's stock exchange, subject to all the ups and downs of the market, but likely to be quoted at some price. However, the preceding generation of novelists translated into individual experience an unusual wealth of ideas from psychology, anthropology, science, and philosophy; the second generation of the century has had to live with their hand-me-down world, modified, but not overturned. We may therefore be living in one of those backwash periods of literary history that the textbooks of 2263 will get over quickly. Nevertheless, we are living in it and in the meantime need to know our resources and liabilities. The insights of our best novelists are one mode of such knowledge. Since we run no risk of holding an inflated opinion of our age, we are entitled not to downgrade it offhandedly.

Though modern criticism has in theory put the work over the author, it has not only maintained, but vastly extended, the personalist emphasis upon a writer's total output as compared to individual works. Dickens is a major novelist, Charlotte Brontë a minor one. Yet few would rank *A Tale of Two Cities* or *Oliver Twist* above *Villette*. In spite of current claims for Lawrence, *Aaron's Rod* is inferior to many novels of the century—certainly to Forster's *Howard's End* or Green's *Concluding* or Powell's *A Buyer's Market*. I am not arguing, of course, against Dickens, Lawrence, or the idea of the major writer, but for an awareness of what the personalist emphasis means. *Intruder in the Dust* may help us understand Faulkner's development, may throw light on his earlier novels, and may by extension tell us something about other contemporary writers; but it is not as good a novel as Saul Bellow's *The Adventures of Augie March*. If quality is the issue, the best works of "minor" writers are better than all but the best works of major ones. The specialist often has his own reasons for concentrating on established figures, but the reader who reads for the work itself loses by ignoring the lesser writers.

One of the fascinations, too, about dealing with immediately contemporary literature is its plasticity. A mythology of grandeur surrounds the great names from the past, making them difficult to move about for reinterpretation. Cruxes, answers, and evaluations become fixed. No such heroic history protects the immediate contemporary. We do not even know whether we have asked the relevant questions. Given twenty-five years, an age is usually right about its best writers and partly right, at least, about interpreting them. The competition and theories sort themselves out. The majority of the novelists in this book, however, have not gone through that twenty-five years.

What, then, do these novelists have to say? The question could be unanswerable, but in this case there are some common denominators. The only catch is that what *they* have to say is less significant than what each *he* has to say.

THE RAPID OBSOLESCENCE OF VALUES

My main concern is the particular human image and situation to which each novelist gives form. Nevertheless, since these comic novelists have written within a single culture and a limited period, their common interests reflect some agreement.

Most people believe that we live in a time of unusual terrors, identified at the moment with Russia and missiles. Though this sense doubtless compares itself with the nineteenth century from 1814 on rather than with history in general, it has its kind of truth. But this abstract fear of horrors survived and to be survived does not quite come down to individuals in a day-to-day reality. The comic novels, which do touch this concrete reality, put the major conflicts in another way.

The one reality that all the novelists agree on is a rapid obsolescence of programs. Nineteenth-century comic fiction writers—Jane Austen, Thackeray, Trollope, Meredith—assume natural, if evolutionary, laws of society. Elizabeth Bennett plays her lively game within the rules, her sister Lydia does not— and justice prevails. Becky Sharp tests how far energy and intel-

ligence can go against the laws of society without being curbed.
And so on. Modern comic fiction assumes sudden, incomprehensible shifts in these laws.

But *law* is not really the right word. Ideals and styles shift be-
wilderingly as the comic novel moves from Forster to Huxley
and Waugh, then on to Green, Powell, Hartley, and Cary. Each
comic novel has its cycle of destroying the old values, improvising new ones, and testing their workings. One effect of sudden
historical change—the 1914 war, prosperity, the depression, the
1939 war, and the intensified organization world—has been to
wear out styles and ideals more rapidly than they once wore out,
to create in the individual the sense that the world of his upbringing and youth is not the world he must face today and
tomorrow. Social mobility, with its sense of vaster than usual
distance between childhood and career, adds to this feeling of
unsystematic shocks.

In the comic novels the ideals and styles wear out rapidly because they are improvisations to meet sudden change; before
they can become traditions, events and individual experience
show up their inadequacy. These stopgaps provide the themes of
Huxley, Waugh, and the Henry Green of *Party-Going*. A new
improvisation arises in Green's later work, and, in the most
recent turn, Powell, Hartley, and Cary raise the general issue:
perhaps "humankind cannot bear much reality" if reality means
sudden frustration of long-held aims and constant shifts of program. How can anyone *love* a reality of this sort enough to
commit himself seriously within it? How much and what kind
of "adjustment" can people make, assuming personality to be
fairly well formed in childhood? How well can improvisation,
whose consequence naturally cannot be foreseen, actually work?

This sense of rapid change is more important than the theory
of a God-forsaken world in creating these contemporary fictional
conflicts. An earlier generation faced the lack of agreement on
over-all purpose and meaning in life. The *Wasteland* lament
for a lost community program has evolved into acceptance of
a fact. Henry Adams' Virgin and Dynamo state this static conception as straightforwardly as it can be stated, but Adams' is not
the contemporary novelist's sense of a problem. The contemporary sees something more like an end run, called at the line

of scrimmage, going for twenty yards and then being called back for offside.

If there is anything approaching a common faith, it is that people never really lose their values, but will always be experimenting with the next program as the old one goes down. These novelists challenge the cliché about a general loss. (The cliché itself expresses a religious yearning for unity in a crowded, obstacle-ridden world and so habitually draws its sustenance from Dante. Its exponents seldom mention Chaucer, who shows multiplicity of purpose within an over-all agreement remote from daily life.) Modern comic novelists show an active destruction of some values, their provisional replacement, another destruction, another provisional replacement. In this rhythm, what creates the apparent loss of values is the unspoken nature of the new commitment. The commitment often goes unvoiced because, in the light of the past, it seems disrespectable—stated as idea. Yet characters base their lives on it in default of anything better. One function of the comic novel has been to separate living values from respectable ones. Confusion between the two becomes one of the characters' problems.

For example, neither play nor security is quite respectable as an ideal; but they are and have been living ones. Present-day students—and professors—do "conform" more than those of a generation ago, and for good reasons, though they usually feel rather than articulate the reasons. Such conformists are highly vulnerable to spokesmen for the now respectable past like Irving Howe, who accuses them of spiritlessness. But they are not spiritless; they have merely lived through a personal and cultural history different from that of the intellectuals of the thirties. Their spiritedness takes another direction. Vitality asserts itself in an effort to build a smaller, more personal and familial, hopefully more controllable, world. In doing so they illustrate a point which the comic novel has been making: people stopped in one direction overdevelop another impulse until its limits become clear and unbearable.

Theories based on traditional comedy do not fit contemporary practice too well. Critics who think of comic writers as instinctively conservative cite Shakespeare, Molière, or Jane Austen. On the other hand, Northrop Frye's theory, based on Latin

comedy, emphasizes the victory of youth and the forces of change
over a reluctant older generation. Modern comic novelists are on
both sides. Forster appears to fit the conservative pattern, Cary
the Frye one. Actually they and the rest are of both parties. They
represent an attachment to inertia—habit persisting or recover-
able—*and* to change. Novelists, like other intellectuals of the
century, have been at the front of movements insisting on
change as a value almost in itself—and they have recognized the
formidable appeal of continuity and identity. They have pre-
sented, with varying sympathies, tensions between the two.
Significantly, the happy ending has become more often a wearing out of the tension to a point where it can be met with a wry
face. The problem of integrating past and present goes on.

This process of integration has shifted in the last twenty years
from a group effort to a more personal one. Inconsistency of
purpose in the culture has provided not only the novelist's
tensions, but a set of apparently irrational situations usable as
symbols. The extended opportunity for young men to rise has
established another sense of the absurd present compared to the
formative past. But in real people these social jars act upon pre-
dispositions already present from childhood and adolescence. A
recognition of this persistence has recently created a comedy of
personal rather than communal effort at integration. In different
ways Green, Powell, and Hartley have given a depth to comedy
which the more social form of their predecessors did not try for.
Sociological comedy has evolved toward a comedy of emotional
patterns.

These opening remarks do not, let me repeat, constitute my
thesis about the modern comic novel. They illustrate some common concerns. The process reviewed in the last chapter—a
continuing conversation, with one novelist taking up the problem before another has quite left off, adding his bit, and being replaced—is nearer my understanding of how a live tradition
works. But it works only as each novelist develops a high individuality of his own. The crucial question of the book is
whether such individual accomplishment exists, but two points
of reference—Forster, here cast as the giant before the flood, and
Huxley—will provide some framework.

CHAPTER TWO

Family Reunions

E. M. FORSTER

THE BREAKUP AND continuance of the family are such consistent themes in E. M. Forster's novels that every reader must understand them in a way. But, asked anything specific about them, he is unlikely to understand much more than that they exist, and even less likely to understand their relation to other themes to which critics have given a more prominent place. So my turning Eliot's title to Forster's feeling for family continuity does not mean to be whimsical but to focus an apparent paradox. Most critics of Forster have made much of his liberalism. But, unlike Eliot, the avowed conservative, who in his plays distrusts a return to family roots, Forster in every novel but one uses a sense of family continuity to make reconciliation with the adult world possible. A conservatism about the family sustains his liberalism about other institutions—though *sustains* is a simple word for a more dynamic process.

Roughly, two of Forster's novels are about breaking away from the family, two about trying to restore it, and the fifth about trying to live without it. *Where Angels Fear to Tread* and *A Room with a View* do show rebellions against the passive acceptance of family values. *The Longest Journey* is Ricky's struggle to accept members of his family whom he cannot readily accept—mother, wife, brother—and ends in partial acceptance and a promise of reconciliation in a new generation. *Howard's End* deals with the estrangement of two sisters who are eventually reconciled with another promise of fuller reconciliation in a new generation. *A Passage to India,* his most pessimistic and searching novel, carries the resolution in *Howard's End* through a sterner test and concludes on the most skeptical note about personal relations in Forster. (Margaret's defense of Helen in a crisis—the defense of a social outcast by an uncomfortable member of the comfortable class—leads to a "happy" ending. *A Passage to India* tests the community of spirit induced by an uncomfortable Englishman's defending a Mohammedan doctor in a British Indian court, and finds it successful during the crisis but no basis for understanding because interests diverge too far.)

But each main action has a counteraction. When *Where Angels Fear to Tread* and *A Room with a View* are read only as rebellions in favor of a freer, more natural life, the family becomes a restrictive conspiracy opposing growth and intruding into the hero or heroine's adult life an archaic set of *don't's*. But this restrictiveness is only one side. In both novels the scenes from family life also give a base of habitual affections and resentments on which the Archimedean main figure can stand. And the characters in both novels make more sense as groups than as individuals. By themselves they are startlingly incomplete. In *A Room with a View* George needs Mr. Emerson and his theories for his own brooding naturalism to mean anything, Lucy needs Charlotte and Mr. Beebe to give direction to the passive side of her nature. In Italy Lucy resists some of Charlotte's ideas and is bewildered by others, but Charlotte is Lucy's conscience and is obeyed, disobeyed, liked, and disliked in about the way consciences can expect. Without Charlotte's negatives and hesitations, Lucy would be only the girl who plays Beethoven with a little too much enthusiasm. And if Lucy's marriage to George were a straightforward rebellion against the family *don't's*, she should in all logic slough off Charlotte, who as chaperon constantly reminds Lucy that she speaks for her mother. But, although by *Howard's End* Forster can say that "conversion is an idea peculiarly appealing to half-baked minds," *A Room with a View* ends with two conversions—of Lucy and the chaperon. And active cooperation, not merely passive assent, is required from Charlotte for the marriage to take place. Lucy and George, separated by misunderstandings, can be married only when Charlotte has been converted to the fuller life and passively conspires in the arrangements with Mr. Emerson.

A similar conversion of the chaperon happens in *Where Angels Fear to Tread*. Philip finds a freer, more natural way of life in Italy, but again the spinster loosely attached to the family must be converted before Philip can believe in his own experience. (Forster, like Mr. Beebe, is a connoisseur of spinsters.) Caroline Abbott, the chaperon who has tried to atone for her previous failure by making sure that Philip carries out the family mission, leads him to see that the "rescue" of Gino's baby is wrong, though Philip has been seeing that in a way all along. The discovery of Italy is a tourist's discovery in both novels and must be absorbed by the more meaningful life in England. It is not enough for Lucy and Philip to rebel. Without the chaperon's participation the rebellion has no standing or promise of endurance. In both his novels about breaking away from the family, Forster's conservatism leads him to carry the family authority along with the rebels.

But these chaperons are not so much "authority" as Forster's special way of by-passing the problems of authority. Since the fathers are dead in his novels, the chaperons are the nearest approaches to moral authority; but, though they have a set of imperatives, they have a happily limited power of enforcing them. Charlotte's position as a poor relation makes her power equivocal, and Caroline and Harriet cannot make Philip do anything. But these spinsters, whose lives are arrested and who ape the older generation, are far sterner than the mothers. The mothers in these novels are more motherly and less saintly than the withdrawn, dying ones in the last two novels. They are comfortable, irritating, complaining, fussy, lovable. Philip's relation with his mother has added the value of a permissive disregard. She gives him a comfortable way of living, nags him, but, except for the trip to Italy, leaves him free to do as he pleases. She objects, but her objections have become conventionalized and can be disregarded without consequence to their relation.

This conservatism about the family even in the novels of rebellion forecasts a stronger conservatism in *Howard's End*.

Howard's End shows the reasons for the breakup of the Schlegel family, the efforts to establish individual ways of life, and the reconciliation on a basis which allows for adult experience. At the beginning of the novel the Schlegel sisters have no problem of breaking away from parents—they are as free as people can be. They have money, friends, intelligence, and apparent stability. The novel treats the further difficulty in personal relations caused by different views of human nature.

Howard's End involves a dichotomy between structure and texture or, to use other terms, between formal and sympathetic structures. Everyone who writes on Forster must respect Lionel Trilling, but Forster's plots are among the most diagrammable in English literature and Trilling's interest in a modulated liberalism makes him emphasize the formal structure of *Howard's End*—intellectual versus businessman versus underdog—at the expense of the sympathetic structure. The truly interested writing in *Howard's End*, like the truly interested writing in Trilling's own *The Middle of the Journey*, is about intellectual versus intellectual—the split between Margaret and Helen over how life should be lived and their reconciliation by including something from both their values. (There is a second, though weaker, kind of vitality in Forster's condescension to Leonard Bast, the clerk who aspires to the Schlegel values, knows he will not achieve them, and becomes morally significant in rejecting a sentimental, quickie view of the possibilities of experience. Leonard cannot achieve anything positive, but he can discover that an all-night walk in the woods is painful, not romantic.)

In saying this I do not mean that a reasonable structure of the novel cannot be set up through the conflict between activist, intellectual, and underdog. But a telling point in a "comedy" of manners is, when is it comic? *Howard's End* can be comic about Leonard's puzzling over Ruskin's "Seven miles to the north of Venice. . . ." But Forster says that the greatest feeling is the sense of space and, by the criterion of free movement, the comic and telling parts of *Howard's End* are in the Schlegels' tone about serious matters. The scene where Margaret urges Tibby to choose a career has this kind of ease. Tibby's significance lies in his commitment to being uncommitted. But Margaret has been thinking of marriage and the Wilcoxes, and would like to impose a little Wilcox spirit on Tibby. What comes out is a community-in-difference:

Did he at all know where he wanted to live? Tibby didn't know that he did know. Did he at all know he wanted to do? He was equally uncertain, but when pressed remarked that he should prefer to be quite free of any profession. Margaret was not shocked, but went on sewing for a few minutes before she replied:

"I was thinking of Mr. Vyse. He never strikes me as particularly happy."

"Ye-es," said Tibby, and then held his mouth open in a curious quiver, as if he, too, had thought of Mr. Vyse, had seen round, through, over, and beyond Mr. Vyse, had weighed Mr. Vyse, grouped him, and finally dismissed him as having no possible bearing on the subject under discussion. That bleat of Tibby's infuriated Helen. But Helen was now down in the dining-room preparing a speech about political economy. At times her voice could be heard declaiming through the floor.

"But Mr. Vyse is rather a wretched, weedy man, don't you think? Then there's Guy. That was a pitiful business. Besides"—shifting to the general—"every one is better for some regular work."

Groans.

"I shall stick to it," she continued, smiling. "I am not saying it to educate you; it is what I really think. I believe that in the last century men have developed the desire for work, and they must not starve it. It's a new desire. It goes with a great deal that's bad, but in itself it's good, and I hope that for women, too, 'not to work' will soon become as shocking as 'not to be married' was a hundred years ago."

"I have no experience of this profound desire to which you allude," enunciated Tibby.

"Then we'll leave the subject till you do. I'm not going to rattle you around. Take your time. Only do think over the lives of the men you like most, and see how they've arranged them."

"I like Guy and Mr. Vyse most," said Tibby faintly, and leant so far back in his chair that he extended in a horizontal line from knees to throat.

But Tibby, apparently downed, sees through Margaret and craftily turns the talk to marriage and the Wilcoxes.

Forster varies his community-in-difference theme skillfully through a scene as different as Helen's story about Mrs. Bast:

As she spoke, the door was flung open, and Helen burst in in a state of extreme excitement.

"Oh, my dears, what do you think? You'll never guess. A woman's been here asking me for her husband. Her what?" (Helen was fond of supplying her own surprise.) "Yes, for her husband, and it really is so."

"Not anything to do with Bracknell?" cried Margaret, who had lately taken on an unemployed of that name to clean the knives and boots.

"I offered Bracknell, and he was rejected. So was Tibby. (Cheer up, Tibby!) It's no one we know. I said, 'Hunt, my good woman; have a good look round, hunt under the tables, poke up the chimney, shake out the antimacassars. Husband? Husband?' Oh, and she so magnificently dressed and tinkling like a chandelier."

"Now, Helen, what did happen really?"

"What I say. I was, as it were, orating my speech. Annie opens the door like a fool, and shows a female straight in on me, with my mouth open. Then we began—very civilly. 'I want my husband, what I have reason to believe is here.' No—how unjust one is. She said 'whom,' not 'what.' She got it perfectly. So I said, 'Name, please?' and she said, 'Lan, Miss,' and there we were."

"Lan?"

"Lan or Len. We were not nice about our vowels. Lanoline."

"But what an extraordinary—"

"I said, 'My good Mrs. Lanoline, we have some grave misunderstanding here. Beautiful as I am, my modesty is even more remarkable than my beauty, and never, never has Mr. Lanoline rested his eyes on mine.'"

"I hope you were pleased," said Tibby.

"Of course," Helen squeaked. "A perfectly delightful experience. Oh, Mrs. Lanoline's a dear—she asked for a husband as if he were an umbrella. She mislaid him Saturday afternoon—and for a long time suffered no inconvenience. But all night, and all this morning her apprehensions grew. Breakfast didn't seem to be the same—no, no more did lunch, and so she strolled up to 2, Wickham Place as being the most likely place for the missing article."

"But how on earth—"

"Don't begin how on earthing. 'I know what I know,' she kept repeating, not uncivilly, but with extreme gloom. In vain I asked her what she did know. Some knew what others knew, and others didn't, and if they didn't, then others again had better be careful. Oh dear, she was incompetent! She had a face like a silkworm, and the dining-room reeks of orris-root. We chatted pleasantly a little about husbands, and I wondered where hers was too, and advised her to go to the police. She thanked me. We agreed that Mr. Lanoline's a notty, notty man, and hasn't no business to go on the lardy-da. But I think she suspected me up to the last."

In comparison, when Forster sets Schlegels against Wilcoxes, the intellectual woman against the new rich, his scenes become angry and he is almost always outside his characters. He is edgy with Charles Wilcox even about Charles' liking for automobiles. He treats Evie's sporting life and Dolly's talk to her child as equal absurdities. He makes Mr. Wilcox foolish for thinking about subletting instead of worrying about Leonard, whom Mr. Wilcox does not know. In showing the new rich, Forster loads the situations so much that the writing becomes satiric and often too irritable to be telling. Right quarrels with wrong, and the reader is uncomfortable with the easy distinction.

The interesting conflict in *Howard's End,* then, is not between right and wrong, but between two rights—which ought to be complementary and are not. Forster portions out between Margaret and Helen attitudes and qualities he admires with a minimum of reservation. Both are right, their tone is right, and the family scenes work in a way that the diagrammable scenes do not. And scenes of the Schlegels with Leonard work, though in a different way.

The family conflict and reconciliation has a structure of its own, with turning points different from those of the class conflict. The novel opens with the family unity upset by Helen's attraction to and quick revulsion from the Wilcoxes. The first part—to the time the Schlegels are forced to leave the house in Wickham Place so that new apartments can be built—shows the family unity being subjected to the strain of interests changing with age. Forster places Margaret's drama at the moment in her life when she is losing interest in the "life of lectures and concerts." She is reluctant to part from the banter and enthusiasm of life at Wickham Place, but her own restiveness is the inner wish which matches the threat from outside—the tearing down of the house in the name of "progress." She wants to make other arrangements, and is being forced to. Her weariness with lectures and concerts comes out explicitly after her marriage.

> As for theatres and discussion societies, they attracted her less and less. She began to "miss" new movements, and to spend her spare time re-reading or thinking, rather to the concern of her Chelsea friends. They attributed the change to her marriage, and perhaps some deep instinct did warn her not to travel further from her husband than was inevitable. Yet the main cause lay deeper still; she had outgrown stimulants, and was passing from words to things. It was doubtless a pity not to keep up with Wedekind or John, but some closing of the gates is inevitable after thirty, if the mind itself is to become a creative power.

At the time Margaret responds both to Mrs. Wilcox's withdrawn quality and to her complete concern with her family. And in marrying Mr. Wilcox later, Margaret works out her lived myth, trying to put herself in the place of a mother figure even to the point of marrying the father figure and, like Mrs. Wilcox, feeling uncomfortable everywhere except in the atmosphere of quiet, renewal, and continuity represented by the farm at Howard's End. Entirely aside from the Wilcoxes' cheating, Margaret is not ready to inherit Howard's End at the time Mrs. Wilcox leaves it to her. She can truly inherit it only after she has in her way gone through Mrs. Wilcox's experiences with Mr. Wilcox and worked out a *modus vivendi* suited to her own personality. She never feels comfortable with Mr. Wilcox. He is always the problem, to be handled by a compromise of good sense but never accepted as the ideal father which Margaret's talk about her own father and her decision to marry imply she is searching for. She is still talking about her own father near the end of the novel.

The basis for estrangement between Helen and Margaret is set up in the opening scenes, which seem at the time to lead toward greater solidarity. Helen at first likes the sense of masculine sureness which the Wilcoxes all apparently have. But she can live with this assurance only so long as she believes it to be complete. Every man should be ideally courageous, every woman ideally beautiful. Helen is not ideally beautiful, but she holds Paul to a standard of ideal courage and, when she sees him as the frightened son in a patriarchal system, feels betrayed and rejects all Wilcoxes totally. Aunt Juley's blundering rescue brings Helen back to the family and Aunt Juley's argument that Schlegels are better than Wilcoxes, foolishly carried on and foolishly answered, still makes Helen's point.

Margaret supports Helen in her flight from the Wilcoxes. But she herself comes on them from another side and her friendship with Mrs. Wilcox is an enthusiasm not shared by Helen or their intellectual friends. The estrangement between the sisters arises from a divergence of sympathies rather than quarrels of the Lawrence sort. They do what people with ideals about "personal relations" can to smooth over the divergence, but Helen rejects the managing, authoritarian spirit so thoroughly that she can like only the underdog Leonard Bast. Trying to hold to the existing arrangement, she opposes Margaret's marriage violently:

> "Don't," sobbed Helen, "don't, don't, Meg, don't!" She seemed incapable of saying any other word. Margaret, trembling herself, led her forward up the road, till they strayed through another gate on to the down.
>
> "Don't, don't do such a thing! I tell you not to—don't! I know—don't!"
>
> "What do you know?"
>
> "Panic and emptiness," sobbed Helen. "Don't!"
>
> Then Margaret thought, "Helen is a little selfish. I have never behaved like this when there has seemed a chance of her marrying." She said: "But we would still see each other very often, and—"
>
> "It's not a thing like that," sobbed Helen. And she broke right away and wandered distractedly upwards, stretching her hands towards the view and crying.
>
> "What's happened to you?" called Margaret, following through the wind that gathers at sundown on the northern slopes of the hills. "But it's stupid!" And suddenly stupidity seized her, and the immense landscape was blurred. But Helen turned back.
>
> "Meg—"
>
> "I don't know what's happened to either of us," said Margaret, wiping her eyes. "We must have both gone mad." Then Helen wiped hers, and they even laughed a little.

Forster says that Helen's brief affair with Leonard is loveless, a combination of impulse and principle. But in the earlier scenes at Wickham Place Helen takes a different interest in him from Margaret's. Margaret tries to deal humanely with his immediate problem, but takes no great personal interest. Helen baits him, jokes at him when she knows he cannot answer in kind.

> An air of evasion characterized Mr. Bast. He explained again, but was obviously lying, and Helen didn't see why he should get off. She had the cruelty of youth. Neglecting her sister's pressure, she said, "I still don't understand. When did you say you paid this call?"
>
> "Call? What call?" said he, staring as if her question had been a foolish one, a favourite device of those in midstream.
>
> "This afternoon call."
>
> "In the afternoon, of course!" he replied, and looked at Tibby to see how the repartee went. But Tibby, himself a repartee, was unsympathetic, and said, "Saturday afternoon or Sunday afternoon?"
>
> "S—Saturday."
>
> "Really!" said Helen; "and you were still calling on Sunday, when your wife came here. A long visit."
>
> "I don't call that fair," said Mr. Bast, going scarlet and handsome. There was fight in his eyes. "I know what you mean, and it isn't so."
>
> . . . "Mr. Bast, you're a born adventurer," laughed Margaret. "No professional athlete would have attempted what you've done. It's a wonder your walk didn't end in a broken neck. Whatever did your wife say?"
>
> "Professional athletes never move without lanterns and compasses," said Helen. "Besides, they can't walk. It tires them. Go on."
>
> "I felt like R.L.S. You probably remember how in 'Virgini-bus—' "
>
> "Yes, but the wood. This 'ere wood. How did you get out?"

But Helen becomes obsessed with the idea that something must be done for him. Her illusion is that a mothering, instinctive helpfulness can triumph over all the "little things" that thwart Leonard and separate him and her as people. She and he have both been let down by the practical, managing people, by Margaret as well as by the Wilcoxes.

For Margaret's marriage to Mr. Wilcox is not merely an identification with Mrs. Wilcox or a desperate determination to be protected by a fatherly man. She and Mr. Wilcox deserve each other in another way. They are both managers of life and the emotions rather than followers of them. The main threat of the novel is not, as Trilling says, that the Wilcoxes may inherit England, but that they may inherit Margaret. She feels this threat herself and sees the marriage as one of opposites in which she must maintain a willingness to compromise, but also keep her individuality.

> By quiet indications the bridge would be built and span their lives with beauty.
> But she failed. For there was one quality in Henry for which she was never prepared, however much she reminded herself of it: his obtuseness. He simply did not notice things, and there was no more to be said. He never noticed that Helen and Frieda were hostile, or that Tibby was not interested in currant plantations; he never noticed the lights and shades that exist in the greyest conversation, the finger-posts, the milestones, the collisions, the illimitable views.

From the point of view of the novel, Margaret's commitment to Mr. Wilcox is wrong, but real. To preserve it she refuses Helen's arguments after the discovery of Mr. Wilcox's affair with Jackie, and the estrangement from Helen, hitherto kept within bounds, becomes an actual separation.

> They spent their honeymoon near Innsbruck. Henry knew of a reliable hotel there, and Margaret hoped for a meeting with her sister. In this she was disappointed. As they came south, Helen retreated over the Brenner, and wrote an unsatisfactory postcard from the shores of the Lake of Garda, saying that her plans were uncertain and had better be ignored. Evidently she disliked meeting Henry. Two months are surely enough to accustom an outsider to a situation which a wife has accepted in two days, and Margaret had again to regret her sister's lack of self-control. In a long letter she pointed out the need of charity in sexual matters: so little is known about them; it is hard enough for those who are personally touched to judge; then how futile must be the verdict of Society. . . . Helen thanked her for her kind letter—rather a curious reply. She moved south again, and spoke of wintering in Naples.

Helen settles in Germany and conceals her pregnancy because she can no longer count on complete sympathy from Margaret.

My point so far is that Forster's imagination is more fully engaged when he writes about the articulate and self-conscious members of an intellectual family than when he writes about people who, whether for Leonard's or Mr. Wilcox's reasons, are less articulate and self-conscious. But the point would hold true further: he writes better about Aunt Juley than about Evie or Charles Wilcox, though both are more important to the formal structure of the novel than she is. These second-generation Wilcoxes, the furthest remove from the Schlegel sisters' concern with the complexities of experience and their own natures, are puppets illustrating arrogance, jealousy, suspicion, and cupidity. But it would be foolish to deny Forster's interest in his class conflict. A page count would prove that even if the text did not insist on it. So the serious question becomes, what is the relation between the class conflict and the family conflict?

Again roughly, Forster's major tension is between the desire to shape life by what seems best and possible in the present and the desire to maintain the meaning of the formative past. The Schlegel sisters want to master the adult world and yet keep the child's sense of identity and continuity. Such balances seldom come out even, but Forster's individuality shows most in the way he tries to balance. The conflict of Wilcoxes, Schlegels, and Basts establishes the primary moral line—tells us what value to put on people with sharply different temperaments and aims. The action of the novel rewards and punishes in these terms. Margaret and Helen, who provide the moral center of this drama, inherit and live at Howard's End. The second-generation Wilcoxes are routed. Charles is imprisoned, all are separated permanently from their father. Mr. Wilcox, the patriarch, is shorn—for defending his children's and his own rules of conduct against Margaret's. Charles' killing Leonard with the old sword caricatures the Wilcox claim to descent from the warrior class as well as the Schlegel ideal of the warrior-philosopher. Charles has overrated himself and Margaret has been tempted to overrate Mr. Wilcox. The ending is a *Jane Eyre* one: the offenders are punished severely and the husband is gelded, needing thereafter only a nurse. Conversely, Leonard, who could never fit in at Howard's End but wanted to, is given an absurd but good death while trying to do a last "right thing." The Schlegel sisters inherit because they have deserved to, but the high barriers to community of spirit remain barriers. Helen and Margaret both try to reach understanding with people of extremely different backgrounds, temperaments, and hopes. The novel yields no ground at all to this possibility.

But all this was in the cards, though the reader does not see that until the end. Too great differences are separative and, at close quarters, produce only the urge to destroy or an ineffective sympathy. But the drama of estrangement and reconciliation within the family cannot be resolved by an either/or. The Schlegel sisters have enough understanding and sympathy to make for some solidarity. But both for a time face a feeling of uprootedness, of self-searching, that makes their own activities and their friends' seem superficial. Their decisions during this period come from sympathies, hitherto submerged, toward people outside their group. They want to identify with people who are different, but they do not agree on different-in-what-way. Their alienation is built up slowly and comes to a crisis through their acting on these submerged sympathies. Margaret goes along with Mr. Wilcox and sees that he cannot be a rescuer for Leonard Bast. Helen believes that he is Leonard's destroyer. She asks that a man whose life and aspirations are drastically out of kilter be put right by individual responsibility and action.

So in the more personal conflict the outsiders, Wilcox and Bast, become objects of attraction fitting Margaret's and Helen's immediate needs. But since they do not successfully work as protector and protégé—Margaret is caring for Henry at the end, Helen "cannot love a man"—they contribute to a reconciliation only in an oblique way. The question can fairly be raised whether the characters who fit the primary moral line of the novel have a lasting part in the lives of the more self-aware characters.

But they do. In the end the family is reconstituted on a new basis. One way is, of course, by exclusion. Of those belonging before, Aunt Juley, with her nominal position as the senior

Schlegel, and Tibby, with his indifference and limited possibilities, have dropped out. Of those who might have become members, Mr. Wilcox has been subdued and Leonard had already
been excluded by his own limitations before his death. The child
is the symbolic reminder, though, that Leonard has been meaningful. Margaret has come into her delayed inheritance from
Mrs. Wilcox not only by physically taking over Howard's End,
but by accepting Mrs. Wilcox's sense of experience. She has been
Margaret's example of an independence arising from a sense of
what she is and what is possible for her, combined with a toler-
ance for others' feelings. Mrs. Wilcox rejects Margaret's letter
about Helen early in the novel without rejecting Margaret herself. By the end Margaret has found that, for her, there can be no
such thing as being protected, though she can help to defend
Helen. She achieves her kind of independence backed by her
sense of reliving, but reliving in a "fairer" way, the life of Mrs.
Wilcox in Mrs. Wilcox's own home, where the physical symbols
constantly remind her that such a life is possible. Early in their
relation Margaret tries to express the meaning behind one of
Mrs. Wilcox's unexpandable ideas on life:

> "I almost think you forget you're a girl."
> Margaret was startled and a little annoyed. "I'm twenty-nine,"
> she remarked. "That's not so wildly girlish."
> Mrs. Wilcox smiled.
> "What makes you say that? Do you mean that I have been gauche
> and rude?"
> A shake of the head. "I only meant that I am fifty-one, and that
> to me both of you—Read it all in some book or other; I cannot put
> things clearly."
> "Oh, I've got it—inexperience. I'm not better than Helen, you
> mean, and yet I presume to advise her."
> "Yes. You have got it. Inexperience is the word."
> "Inexperience," repeated Margaret, in serious yet buoyant tones.
> "Of course, I have everything to learn—absolutely everything—
> just as much as Helen. Life's very difficult and full of surprises. At
> all events, I've got as far as that. To be humble and kind, to go
> straight ahead, to love people rather than pity them, to remember
> the submerged—well, one can't do all these things at once, worse
> luck, because they're so contradictory. It's then that proportion

comes in—to live by proportion. Don't begin with proportion. Only prigs do that. Let proportion come in as a last resource, when the better things have failed, and a deadlock—Gracious me, I've started preaching!"

"Indeed, you put the difficulties of life splendidly," said Mrs. Wilcox, withdrawing her hand into the deeper shadows. "It is just what I should have liked to say about them myself."

Later, old Miss Avery, in her clairvoyant confusion, insists on Margaret's obligation to a renewal which will set things right:

"Mrs. Wilcox, it has been mistake upon mistake for fifty years. The house is Mrs. Wilcox's and she would not desire it to stand empty any longer."

To help the poor decaying brain, Margaret said:

"Yes, Mrs. Wilcox's house, the mother of Mr. Charles."

"Mistake upon mistake," said Miss Avery. "Mistake upon mistake."

"Well, I don't know," said Margaret, sitting down in one of her own chairs. "I really don't know what's to be done." She could not help laughing.

The other said: "Yes, it should be a merry house enough."

"I don't know—I dare say. Well, thank you very much, Miss Avery. Yes, that's all right. Delightful."

"There is still the parlour." She went through the door opposite and drew a curtain. Light flooded the drawing-room and the drawing-room furniture from Wickham Place. "And the dining room." More curtains were drawn, more windows were flung open to the spring. "Then through here—" Miss Avery continued passing and repassing through the hall. Her voice was lost, but Margaret heard her pulling up the kitchen blind. "I've not finished here yet," she announced, returning. "There's still a deal to do. The farm lads will carry your great wardrobes upstairs, for there is no need to go into expense at Hilton." . . .

"You think you won't come back to live here, Mrs. Wilcox, but you will."

"That remains to be seen," said Margaret, smiling. "We have no intention of doing so for the present. We happen to need a much larger house. Circumstances oblige us to give big parties. Of course, some day—one never knows, does one?"

Miss Avery retorted: "Some day! Tcha! Tcha! Don't talk about some day. You are living here now."

"Am I?"

"You are living here, and have been for the last ten minutes, if you ask me."

It was a senseless remark, but with a queer feeling of disloyalty Margaret rose from her chair.

And, in the shotgun communion which reconciles Margaret and Mr. Wilcox, Margaret accepts the necessity of earning the meaning of her predecessor's experience:

> Then it was Dolly's turn. Anxious to contribute, she laughed nervously, and said: "Good-bye, Mr. Wilcox. It does seem curious that Mrs. Wilcox should have left Margaret Howard's End, and yet she got it, after all." . . .
>
> Margaret saw their visitors to the gate. Then she returned to her husband and laid her head in his hands. He was pitiably tired. But Dolly's remark had interested her. At last she said: "Could you tell me, Henry, what was that about Mrs. Wilcox having left me Howard's End?"
>
> Tranquilly he replied: "Yes, she did. But that is a very old story. When she was ill and you were so kind to her she wanted to make you some return, and, not being herself at the time, scribbled 'Howards End' on a piece of paper. I went into it thoroughly, and, as it was clearly fanciful, I set it aside, little knowing what my Margaret would be to me in the future."
>
> Margaret was silent. Something shook her life in its inmost recesses, and she shivered.
>
> "I didn't do wrong, did I?" he asked, bending down.
>
> "You didn't, darling. Nothing has been wrong."

But Forster's feeling for the contradictoriness of experience enters in even here. Margaret values most in herself a capacity for decision based on a broad and humane understanding of experience. But in dealing with the arbitrary authority of Mr. Wilcox, she wins by an impulsiveness that is like Helen's. The impulse is not finally inconsistent, but it overrides her immediate principle of give-and-take because Mr. Wilcox will not give as he takes. For Margaret, the action of the novel means discovering, under the stress of change in herself and her circumstances, what she wants and does not want to do.

For Helen, the action reveals what her generous impulsiveness can and cannot do. Her effort to mother Leonard fails, but she can mother the child and can enter into the promise he represents. The pessimism about the great barriers of class and background prevails, though mitigated. Helen and Margaret both find that they can live with another person whose values are similar no matter how great the temperamental difference— and that temperamental differences can be complementary. But neither could have known this with certainty without the attempts at the impossible combination. Both find events and people more inflexible and more unpredictable than they had believed, and return to earlier loyalties. For all the talk about personal relations, the novel is not optimistic about the possibility of having them with people outside the group who have been reared to have similar values. The "inner life" has more inflexible rules than either Margaret or Helen had hoped, but at the end they are prepared to live with this inflexibility in themselves and other people as they were not willing to in the beginning. The novel looks toward the permanent separation between people of *A Passage to India;* the fates of Leonard and Mr. Wilcox are real and forceful. But this pessimism goes along with the concluding scene of stable family life. A family of two middle-aging women, an old man, and a child is a limited prospect, but it fulfills the urgency in the novel to re-establish the threatened unity. Margaret has lost her uprootedness and established a feeling of continuity. Helen has stopped being the outcast she has chosen to be and the Wilcoxes have obligingly treated her as, and begins to think of "such a crop of hay as never."

Treating the Wilcoxes and Leonard Bast in relation to the Schlegel sisters perhaps obscures a qualitative difference. Leonard's interest as a character comes from a brilliant double vision. In one view he is the man blundering toward understanding and culture, an understanding and culture which Forster allows the reader to take for granted as his own. But the barrier is permanent and this is a promised land Leonard can never enter. His interest comes from his desire and his inability to do so. But in most of Forster's work two moral views are honored: one would lead toward the fuller, more natural life, and one would recognize what is not natural to the individual. For Leonard, Ruskin is unnatural. And this negative vision is of the highest importance because so much of ordinary life assumes that everything is possible for anyone. In *A Room with a View* Forster gives a measure of credit to Cecil for recognizing the necessities of his personality. Tibby gets similar credit in *Howard's End*, but in both cases there is too little struggle, the acceptance comes too readily, to create a rounded character. The special combination of affection and irony that Forster has for Leonard is one of his best achievements.

Mr. Wilcox does not measure up to the role the novel demands of him. It is never clear that he has even as much character as Margaret sees in him. He is the creature of her need and Forster's hostility. But one quality of the Wilcoxes as a group does contribute to the novel. I have treated the second-generation Wilcoxes as puppets and they are, but as a family they have an inverted vitality. Their confidence in their rules and actions is enough to diminish Margaret from a flexible to a completely rebellious personality. They have a capacity for making Margaret not herself, but the problem they see her to be. The episode about running over the cat is the grosser treatment of this, but almost any passage where Margaret is with them shows this ability, which, more than anything else, leads to Margaret's shift from compromise to rebellion in the final scenes. She rebels directly against Mr. Wilcox when he and Charles insist on classifying Helen as merely another problem to be handled with a morally timid firmness.

Camus' book *The Rebel* distinguishes between rebellion, which everyone engages in, and revolt, which he symbolizes in the French revolutionaries' step of killing the king. There is a great deal of revolt in Forster's novels, notably in his treatment of Mr. Wilcox. But over-all his chief characters are rebels. In *Where Angels Fear to Tread* the hero comes to a changed view of the possibilities of life; in *A Room with a View* a changed view leads to a change of status, a romantic marriage. But, in both, the main characters want to modify the family authority rather than dispense with it. In *Howard's End* the desire for family continuity causes the revolt against an outside authority.

But the reconciliation between Helen and Margaret comes as they arrange the books, the furniture, and the old sword from Wickham Place at Howard's End. Their common memories and attitudes unite them just before the final quarrel with Mr. Wilcox:

> "But the chairs show up wonderfully. Look where Tibby spilt the soup."
> "Coffee. It was coffee surely."
> Helen shook her head. "Impossible. Tibby was far too young to be given coffee at that time."
> "Was father alive?"
> "Yes."
> "Then you're right and it must have been soup. I was thinking of much later—that unsuccessful visit of Aunt Juley's, when she didn't realize that Tibby had grown up. It was coffee then, for he threw it down on purpose. There was some rhythm, 'Tea, coffee—coffee, tea,' that she said to him every morning at breakfast. Wait a minute—how did it go?"
> "I know—no, I don't. What a detestable boy Tibby was!"
> "But the rhyme was simply awful. No decent person could have put up with it."
> "Ah, that greengage tree," cried Helen, as if the garden was also part of their childhood. "Why do I connect it with dumbbells? And there come the chickens. The grass wants cutting. I love yellow-hammers—"
> Margaret interrupted her. "I have got it," she announced.
>
> > " 'Tea, tea, coffee, tea,
> > Or chocolaritee!'
>
> "That every morning for three weeks. No wonder Tibby was wild."
> "Tibby is moderately a dear now," said Helen.
> "There! I knew you'd say that in the end. Of course he's a dear."

The sisters quarrel because they are what they are, but the hostility toward alien authority and the ineffective sympathy for the underdog are both resolved in family terms—a dependent husband for Margaret, a child for Helen. The rebellion and sympathy which make up Forster's liberalism are enveloped by the theme of family continuity.

There are other implications in these reunions, of course. One is the strong feminine identification in all the novels of manners. Too, Forster's way of using the past has, as Mann would say, its dark side. He often does not incorporate an understanding of the past into the present so that the present can be lived more effectively, as some recent novelists do, but rather in *Howard's End* comes close to using the past as a resistance to the present. At times Margaret and Helen are nearer a frantic effort to restore the older family pattern than they are to understanding. Forster's conservatism about the family works on one hand to deepen the sense of identity and reality. But it also leads to the distrust of experience which is so strong in *A Passage to India*. *A Passage to India* is based not on the tension between restrictiveness and the natural life, but upon fear of attack. The distinction between reality and fantasy is less clearly maintained than in the novels of manners. The melodramatic side of the novel treats fears as representative reality. And it is by too much design that the spinster initiates the attack and is capable of conversion only to the negative honesty of a Leonard Bast.

CHAPTER THREE

The Appeal to Grandfathers

ALDOUS HUXLEY

As a point of reference, then, Forster represents a domesticated romanticism, lived with long enough to seem more homey than revolutionary. He faces what natural man can mean in an urban and suburban society, and finds prototypes in the moody Socialist George Emerson, his plain-speaking father, and the corrupted natural man, Leonard Bast. In *The Longest Journey* Forster idealizes pastoral and primitive. He can capitalize and grow lyrical about the Earth. In his stories he tries to establish Greece, the home of classicism, as a magical, romantic country; in the novels he has more success with Italy as a symbol for the lively, the uninhibited, the expressive.

But Forster faced an unpleasant dilemma about this tradition: much of Victorianism is also domesticated romanticism, and its manners at least are unsatisfactory to him. Victorian novels show these manners as part of a middle-class aspiration to the aristocratic. They reflect a wish for invulnerability to any charge of grossness, natural enough in inheritors building on a rougher generation's achievement. Since Forster wants his romanticism to have the strength of tradition, he meets the problem in *Howard's End* by making it German. Mr. Schlegel, though dead, echoes through the novel as the warrior-philosopher. Helen's long soliloquy on the goblins in the Fifth Symphony is Forster's finest set piece of domestication, as Leonard's walk in the woods at night is his best on romantic ideals in the city. In both episodes Forster wants to think of culture as lived with, not acquired by hard work. (Eliot and Pound, who matured in the Theodore Roosevelt era, think of acquiring the world's culture as very hard work.) This hope for natural continuity obviously does not descend to the postwar novelists, though a nostalgia for it does.

There are several candidates for the title of the Last Victorian, but among the comic novelists Aldous Huxley is the last to take Matthew Arnold seriously—seriously enough, that is, to try turning him upside down. Huxley does show an aspiration to the best that has been thought and known, and also shows considerable acquaintance with it. And, for all his determined modernity, he builds on Forster's logic. *Howard's End* treats a small group of intellectuals trying to come to terms with the active forces in the society, and failing. Huxley accepts this failure as final, and concentrates his test of new hopes on the avant-gardists alone. A family *chosen* by common interest rather than the natural family becomes his unit.

We find it hard nowadays to give Huxley due historical credit. He is less skillful than Waugh, Green, Hartley, and Powell, but he was an innovator. More than any other single novelist, he invented the coterie that Hemingway, Fitzgerald, Waugh, Green, and Powell take as a focus of experience. He located a scene of reality, laid out an original version of the human problem, and invented type characters who recur in his successors. For all this, his importance as a comic novelist rests on only one work, *Antic Hay,* published in 1922. Its significance lies less in its acute social analysis than in its recognition of a weakness in what Thomas Mann later called the lived myth. That weakness is self-consciousness.

The action of *Antic Hay,* though a great advance over the static house party in *Chrome Yellow,* seems haphazard. At the beginning Gumbril, Jr., quits teaching history in a school and returns to London to make his fortune through Gumbril's Patented Small Clothes (pneumatic underwear for bony men). The real interest starts with the restaurant scene. There the coterie appears, fully developed, as a defense against an indifferent and stuffy society. When Mrs. Viveash, the dying-voice heroine, arrives, the typed cast is all but complete: Lypiatt, the megalomaniac painter and poet; Mercaptan, the cautious hedonist; Shearwater, the dedicated physiologist; Coleman, the bearded satanist; and Gumbril, the man looking for the easy way. After a brief, unsuccessful guilty-conscience episode—a glance at real poverty and illness—the novel moves in the next three sections through its test of avant-garde life. Lypiatt's noisy hopes fall against Mrs. Viveash's indifference, and his confidence in his talent cannot withstand her cool laughter. Gumbril adopts a false beard, becomes the Complete Man, launches his underwear scheme, and tries love and pleasure with Rosie Shearwater and the "pure" Emily. While Shearwater falls in love with Mrs. Viveash, Rosie passes through the hands of Gumbril, Mercaptan, and Coleman. The final section portrays an apparent vacuum. Gumbril abandons Emily to console Mrs. Viveash, and they ride around London at night in a cab assuring themselves that all their acquaintances are as miserable as they are.

The movement is almost as confusing as my summary, but it does give reality to group interaction, and for Huxley group is more real than individual. For all their idiosyncrasies, the characters are strictly representative. They can move only in straight lines, but in doing so they collide with each other. Each character in the end illustrates why his myth will not work; it will not work partly because other people will not allow it to. Mainly, though, the special vision in *Antic Hay* comes from a recognition that the determinedly new standards involve an equivocal relation between past and present.

The opening chapters apparently take the past as a mistake. History for schoolboys is foolish, the chaplain and his religion are foolish, the older generation is foolishly remote from present reality. Yet *Antic Hay*, as it develops, holds one attitude toward the social past—scorn—and another toward the personal past— nostalgia. Gumbril, Jr., thinks in the first chapter of his mother:

> As for Gumbril's mother her diligence had not been dogmatic. She had just been diligently good, that was all. Good; good? It was a word people only used nowadays with a kind of deprecating humourousness. Good. Beyond good and evil? We are all that nowadays. Or merely below them, like earwigs? I glory in the name of earwig. Gumbril made a mental gesture and inwardly declaimed. But good in any case, there was no getting out of that, good she had

been. Not nice, not merely *molto simpatica*—how charmingly and effectively these foreign tags assist one in the great task of calling a spade by some other name!—but good. You felt the active radiance of her goodness when you were near her . . . And that feeling, was that less real and valid than two plus two?

The Reverend Pelvey had nothing to reply. He was reading with a holy gusto of "houses full of all good things which thou fillest not, and wells digged, which thou diggedst not, vineyards and olive trees, which thou plantedst not."

She had been good and she had died when he was still a boy; died—but he hadn't been told that till much later—of creeping and devouring pain. Malignant disease—oh, *caro nome!*

"Thou shalt fear the Lord thy God," said Mr. Pelvey.

Even when the ulcers are benign; thou shalt fear. He had travelled up from school to see her, just before she died. He hadn't known that she was going to die, but when he entered her room, when he saw her lying so weakly in the bed, he had suddenly begun to cry, uncontrollably. All the fortitude, the laughter even, had been hers. And she had spoken to him. A few words only; but they had contained all the wisdom he needed to live by. She had told him what he was, and what he should try to be, and how to be it. And crying, still crying, he had promised that he would try.

He regrets the impossibility of communicating with his father and Porteus, but he admires them. Mrs. Viveash explains her promiscuity in tender terms:

"It isn't only food," said Mrs. Viveash, who had closed her eyes and was leaning back in her corner.

"So I can well believe."

"It's everything. Nothing's the same now. I feel it never will be."

"Never more," croaked Gumbril.

"Never again," Mrs. Viveash echoed. "Never again." There were still no tears behind her eyes. "Did you ever know Tony Lamb?" she asked.

"No," Gumbril answered from his corner. "What about him?"

Mrs. Viveash did not answer. What, indeed, about him? She thought of his very clear blue eyes and the fair bright hair that had been lighter than his brown face. Brown face and neck, red-brown hands; and all the rest of his skin was as white as milk. "I was very fond of him," she said at last. "That's all. He was killed in 1917, just about this time of the year. It seems a very long time ago, don't you think?"

Lypiatt is equally tender toward his past hopes, and even Coleman's black masses suggest the relevance of a faith once held.

Though the characters scorn all social authority, the actual fathers in the novel appear as intelligent, well-meaning men who have found their own enthusiasms, but cannot transmit the secret of finding others to their children. They are withdrawn men who occasionally try to share unsharable interests in Renaissance architecture or medieval Latin poets. But the nostalgic younger generation finds a sadly comic spectacle in its elders' nostalgia. Gumbril Senior designs workmen's cottages, but his interest lies in his magnificent models:

> Mr. Gumbril snorted with indignation. "When I think of Alberti!" And he thought of Alberti—Alberti the noblest Roman of them all, the true and only Roman. For the Romans themselves had lived their own actual lives, sordidly and extravagantly in the middle of a vulgar empire. Alberti and his followers in the Renaissance lived the ideal Roman life. They put Plutarch into their architecture. . . .
> "And when I think of Brunellesschi!" Gumbril Senior went on to remember with passion the architect who had suspended on eight thin flying ribs of marble the lightest of all domes and the loveliest.
> "And when of Michelangelo! The grim enormous apse. . . . And of Wren and of Palladio, when I think of all these—" Gumbril Senior waved his arms and was silent. He could not put into words what he felt when he thought of them.

The reader can see where the new generation gets its myth-making enthusiasm, but the characters themselves see only their rejection of the old. For them the only wisdom their seniors pass down is the necessity of finding one's own way: whereas in Forster, something magical descends from the past through characters like Mrs. Wilcox and Mrs. Moore, in Huxley nothing descends automatically from the personal past. Each character is free to choose his own ideals and standards, but must bear the pain of *knowing* that he is creating himself. This awareness of a self-conscious process is Huxley's most effective insight.

His characters glory in their difference from contemporaries still living within the patterns of the past, but none of them can live without constructing a personal mythology to replace the lost tribal mythology. (This tribal mythology is, of course, always being lost; Huxley's special situation is the unusual degree of loss.) Each character justifies himself by some type from literature, art, or history. Lypiatt appeals to Michelangelo and the Renaissance rounded man; Mercaptan prefers the neoclassic role of the belles lettrist, Crébillon the Younger; Shearwater takes the nineteenth-century man of science; Coleman wants the part of satanist; Rosie Shearwater plays at being great lady to a fairly courtly lover. Only the satanist achieves any success, for his role is to destroy others' beliefs in their roles. Lypiatt has the aspirations of a Michelangelo and none of the power. Mercaptan leaves town when the lady takes him too seriously; Rosie loses her dignity with Coleman; Shearwater pedals his bicycle endlessly collecting sweat to prove what everybody knows as much about as he wants to. Gumbril alone protects himself by *playing* at his myth of the Complete Man and getting along like a civilian —a confidence man with no aim more overreaching than money and pleasure.

So the rebels of the avant-garde try to "make it new" by going backward, just as Pound did, to attitudes less damaged by time and the war than Forster's evolutionary romanticism. The appeal is to universals representing permanent human aspirations—the Byronic hero, the neoclassicist, the satanist, the lady, the scientist. But Huxley does not treat all these attitudes with equal seriousness. Mercaptan, who believes love, literature, and living rooms should be tidy, is merely a center of ridicule. Coleman is primarily the antagonist. Rosie is a lightweight. The main action recounts, with many asides, Lypiatt's and Gumbril's efforts to come to terms with Mrs. Viveash.

This queen of the coterie is the sphinx of her society. Actually, she does not seem very interesting, though the characters and Huxley take her as fascinating. In her sleepiness she asks the riddle that no one can answer, and she kills the unsuccessful in turn. The riddle is simply, what can awaken her from her numbness? What can provide the old hope and excitement? Her question tests the genuineness of all the vulnerable enthusiasms. But, though the reader today is apt to find her affected, bored and boring, she appeals to those characters who need more love than they find in the world at large. She seems to Lypiatt and

Shearwater a promising mother goddess who always rejects. (Gumbril had earlier found her so, but finally accepts her as at least undemanding and unpossessive.) She thus offers an object for masochistic satisfactions. Coleman and Mercaptan, who have other plans, do not need this kind of mother.

Mrs. Viveash has one kind of authority in her role. She has defied all puritanical restrictions without achieving intensity. She is disappointed in the leading hope of the coterie—the program of pleasure-without-pain. Her excuse about a lover lost in the war is so lame that not even Huxley gives it much space, but he does underline deficiency of feeling by several parallels. Rosie's pink décor symbolizes the tameness of her affair with the Complete Man. Mercaptan's sofa, named Crébillon the Younger, stands for his pale amours. The Shearwaters' scenes from married life show routine, irritability, indifference—almost calculated efforts to dislike each other. (Lypiatt's and Shearwater's experiences with Mrs. Viveash show what this indifference, which Huxley treats indulgently, defends against—a love too single-minded and so too vulnerable.)

Huxley manages the action of the novel by the nineteenth-century device of splitting the hero's role. Gumbril, the point of view character, remains the control, but he is a secret sharer with the two fanatics, Lypiatt and Coleman. Huxley shows great sympathy for Lypiatt, the artist who can imagine grandeur but not create it. Michelangelo did what he could and produced the Sistine Chapel; Lypiatt does everything he can and produces "vermouth posters." He tests the ideal of the lived myth and finds a chasm between myth and the possible. Yet he cannot abandon the myth to live with the possible, just as he cannot give up his idealized Mrs. Viveash; and he cannot distinguish between his actual emotions and the intensity he believes he should feel. Some of the most typical comedy in the novel emerges from their conversations together:

"May I kiss you?" he asked after a silence.

Mrs. Viveash turned towards him, smiling agonisingly, her eyebrows ironically lifted, her eyes steady and calm and palely, brightly inexpressive. "If it really gives you any pleasure," she said. "It won't, I may say, to me."

"You make me suffer a great deal," said Lypiatt, and said it so

quietly and unaffectedly, that Myra was almost startled; she was
accustomed, with Casimir, to noisier and more magniloquent prot-
estations.

"I'm very sorry," she said; and, really, she felt sorry. "But I
can't help it, can I?"

"I suppose you can't," he said. "You can't," he repeated and his
voice had now become the voice of Prometheus in his bitterness.
"Nor can tigresses." He had begun to pace up and down the un-
obstructed fairway between his easel and the door; Lypiatt liked
pacing while he talked. "You like playing with the victim," he
went on; "he must die slowly."

Reassured, Mrs. Viveash faintly smiled. This was the familiar
Casimir. So long as he could talk like this, could talk like an old-
fashioned French novel, it was all right; he couldn't really be so
very unhappy. She sat down on the nearest unencumbered chair.

Mrs. Viveash can only make him face the immediate, even
though she would almost like to help him:

> "But I don't laugh," said Mrs. Viveash. On the contrary, she was
> very sorry for him; and, what was more, he rather bored her. For a
> few days, once, she had thought she might be in love with him. His
> impetuosity had seemed a torrent strong enough to carry her away.
> She had found out her mistake very soon. After that he had rather
> amused her: and now he rather bored her. No, decidedly, she
> never laughed. She wondered why she still went on seeing him.
> Simply because one must see some one? or why? "Are you going to
> go on with my portrait?" she asked.
>
> Lypiatt sighed. "Yes," he said, "I suppose I'd better be getting
> on with my work. Work—it's the only thing. 'Portrait of a Ti-
> gress.' " The cynical Titan spoke again. "Or shall I call it, 'Por-
> trait of a Woman who has never been in love'?"
>
> "That would be a very stupid title," said Mrs. Viveash.

Gumbril's role of the unconfident confidence man enables
him to play at the greatness that Lypiatt strives for seriously. The
patented small clothes provide Gumbril with a modest aim accepted in the society, and caricature rather than mythologize his
goals. His beard changes his effect on others—from "weak, silent
man" to man of the world—but he remains knowing and playful, undeceived. His Complete Man is a self-aware image, and a
problem arises only where it is unusable, with Emily. He tries to

live by bantering about the values of the age. He sees in Emily the appeal of tender, "true" love in a pastoral cottage with all the problems of active sexuality removed. She enters his life to the tune of Mozart's G Minor Quintet, and, like it, is

> Pure and unsullied; pure and unmixed, unadulterated. "Not passionate, thank God; only sensual and sentimental." In the name of earwig. Amen. Pure, pure.

But after they have slept together without having intercourse, Gumbril sits with Mrs. Viveash and the more complex note appears:

> He thought of Emily in her native quiet among the flowers; in a cottage altogether too cottagey, with honeysuckles and red ramblers and hollyhocks—though, on second thought, none of them would be blooming yet, would they?—happily, in white muslin, extracting from the cottage piano the easier sections of the Arietta. A little absurd, perhaps, when you consider her like that; but exquisite, but adorable, but pure of heart and flawless in her bright pellucid integrity, complete as a crystal in its faceted perfection. She would be waiting for him, expecting him; and they would walk through the twiddly lanes—or perhaps there would be a governess cart for hire, with a fat pony like a tub on legs to pull it—they would look for flowers in the woods and perhaps he would still remember what sort of noise a white-throat makes; or even if he didn't remember, he could always magisterially say he did. "That's a white-throat, Emily. Do you hear? The one that goes 'Tweedly, weedly, weedledy dee.'"
> "I'm waiting," said Mrs. Viveash. "Patiently, however."
> Gumbril looked at her and found her smiling like a tragic mask.

The comic tone imposes that not-quite-tragic mask on the dream of picnicking with Emily. Apparently by accident, Gumbril chooses Mrs. Viveash instead.

Coleman, on the other hand, brutally cuts through the pretensions that Gumbril indulges. The passive Gumbril takes pleasure in Coleman's teasing Shearwater, playing with Zoë, dismissing Mercaptan, and carrying off Rosie. Coleman shows that Mercaptan is a coward, Lypiatt a fool, Shearwater an irrelevancy—and Gumbril agrees with all these estimates. Coleman wants to prove sex apelike, untidy. To Gumbril he seems grounded on the rock of no pretensions beyond his own energy, triumphantly male without the complications of love. Yet Coleman, too, is playing—at turning Christian virtue upside down. He is radically aggressive, aware of every weak spot in others' armor of myth, elevating his negatives to apparent invulnerability. Gumbril thinks him ridiculous and admirable. But even Coleman does not test his aggressiveness against Mrs. Viveash's riddle of apathy.

Together and in action, the three leading male characters provide a chart of possible programs—Lypiatt's in the clouds, Coleman's at bedrock, Gumbril's between. Gumbril remains the control character because he tries to sidestep the romantic, neoclassic, and nihilist attitudes. Shearwater, whom earlier critics took seriously, is actually so easy a mark as to be neither character nor social issue. He is beaten the moment he speaks for kidneys. Everyone knows his scientism is irrelevant. The earnest man trying to disregard sex becomes a moral lesson readily absorbed.

The haphazard action, then, falls into two main lines: in the first Lypiatt overreaches and fails; in the second, Gumbril finds a partial answer to the sphinx's riddle. In the last section of the novel, Gumbril and Mrs. Viveash choose each other, more for worse than for better. Her self-conscious melancholy is more real to him than Emily's honeysuckle-and-roses love. Even in a vacuum of active affection, they do reach a kind of community. Gumbril and Mrs. Viveash deserve each other. The scene in which she urges him to keep talking while she nods off is their consummation: he courts her in a permanent Grecian Urn living room, where wit suffices for love-making and no disgrace attends inability to rouse the unrousable. Their standoff is an agreement. The monster skit in the night club pictures sex as an unfeeling transaction, a foredoomed series of rejections and disappointments. But Mrs. Viveash is real to Gumbril because she too seems bedrock. Rosie, who is playing out of her depth, has not seemed real. Emily's childlike tenderness can exist only in a cottage outside the adult, city world. But Mrs. Viveash guarantees that she has tried everything and everybody, and that nothing works. Her experience gives her the power to absolve Gumbril—and, by extension, the novel—from the unrealizable hopes of each character's private myth. Efforts that lead to delusion might better not be made, she seems to say—and the step from this to Huxley's later interest in the passive religions of the East is not far. What Gumbril does best is talk wittily; what Mrs. Viveash, with her dying voice and inability to give, sympathize, or control, does best is sleep. In their relation each can operate at the top of his bent.

So Gumbril and Mrs. Viveash achieve a communion of sorts on their "last ride together" by finding how uncomfortable the mythmakers are. Readers usually like this part of the novel, perhaps because they are laughing at someone else. The joke is on the mythmakers, not on Gumbril and Mrs. Viveash, who have achieved awareness. They have accepted the gap between myth and reality; unlike the imagery in the *Wasteland,* the recognition brings no sense of urgency. Their comfortable pessimism is all the more comfortable because the joke is on the activists. Lypiatt lies in the dark thinking of suicide; Coleman has just raped Rosie, to her delight and shame; Shearwater bicycles on a treadmill. Talkative passivity has justified itself by negating all action. Gumbril and Mrs. Viveash have achieved the inverse superiority of knowing and not wanting.

Antic Hay, then, brings the test of the ridiculous to newly constructed, hence vulnerable, ideals. It embodies an anesthetic awareness of *nada.* (*The Sun Also Rises,* written a few years later, does not resemble Huxley's novel by chance.) But the novel operates on a sizable letter of credit from the Edwardian world. There are values still around, it suggests, that may deceive the unwary, who must be made wary. *Antic Hay* is one of the pleasanter destructive works, and one of the more sweeping programs for reducing pain.

Critics trying to account for Huxley's failure to achieve more than he does often say that he is primarily an essayist. The undeveloped possibilities—more sensuous immediacy, deeper involvement between the characters, more conflict, more interest in motive, larger ideas of the human range—do make Huxley's writing thinner than the best novelists'. But he does dramatize, in passages like those between Lypiatt and Mrs. Viveash, a conflict between a cold woman who acknowledges her coldness and a cold man who will not acknowledge his, two egoists trying to make egotism a bond. The man's conviction that he *should* have strong emotions makes his talk false. The woman's lack of faith in obligatory intensity shows him up, but her self-pity allows her to extend only a little sympathy. It is real conflict, with a second convolution. The reader's awareness of other novelists may make him ask for more, but Huxley does dramatize two previously undiagnosed senses of experience, and the accomplishment is neither essayist nor negligible.

In essence, Huxley maps the world instead of visiting its more complex scenes—crosses off legendary continents that do not exist and pinpoints islands that do. His characters plot their bearings by remote stars and follow a fixed course over the horizon. They do not change much with experience or develop illogical traits, but work out the order of destinies implicit from their first appearance. This vision of human nature as oddly logical rather than deeply contradictory makes for thinness—and shock.

Another reason for the thinness in *Antic Hay* is Huxley's comic mode itself. To keep a center of sanity in a coterie of fanatics, he has his narrator play at having the disease while really suffering no more than the after-effects of vaccination. The power of *Antic Hay* comes from the opening third, which plots the bearings, and the last third, which shows the characters sailing straight over the horizon. But since Gumbril is not going on this trip, the middle section about his affair with Rosie and his talks on advertising inevitably seem less real than the stories of the committed characters.

This combination of inventive beginnings with orderly development makes for Huxley's most popular work. People who have never heard of *Point Counter Point* or *These Barren Leaves* like *Brave New World*. Though it is a satire and does not come strictly within a discussion of the comic novel, it succeeds precisely because the reader's view of the future is also thin and logical. Our visions of the future naturally do what Huxley always does—map a few points and expect "the logic of the present" to fulfil itself logically.

The conflict in *Brave New World* centers about freedom and its important corollary, play. The projected logic says that, instead of trying to live by self-conscious myths, the world will hereafter live by "rational" planning for pleasure, with all saving pain eliminated. The undifferentiated characters enjoy their free love and avoid involvements; but the one differentiated character in the early part—another uncomfortable member of the comfortable classes—speaks for a conscience which the new values bring into the open. (Bernard Marx is a sort of self-aware Lypiatt, without Lypiatt's ambiguity and exhibitionism.) For at least one hundred and fifty years people have believed themselves obligated to feel more intense emotions than their ancestors wanted to, but the period after the first World War applied this conscience to sex more single-mindedly than preceding romantics had done. Bernard Marx would like to feel as intensely as Heathcliffe, but since nothing in the environment frustrates him, he cannot, according to his theory, feel the pain which conscience tells him he should; yet he cannot enjoy the "pneumatic" girls as much as his colleagues say they do.

Through Bernard the novel lets the reader have the best of both worlds, lets him enjoy the fun and yet feel superior to the unfallen pleasure-seekers. But, for all Bernard's contribution, admirers of *Brave New World* do not remember him too well. They remember the sentimental Savage better, and remember most of all the magnificent rationality applied to reducing pain and producing pleasure. Compared to *1984*, *Brave New World* shows amazing confidence in peaceful, orderly social development, and does not foresee the coercions and crises that have beset later decades. The memorable parts of the satire show the assembly line births; the available girls, with their polished Malthusian belts; *soma*, the drug that substitutes joy for anxiety; the sleep-conditioning with its moral messages like "everybody belongs to everybody else;" and the children taught sex play at nursery school. From the ostensible moral point of view the wrong things excite the novelist's, and the reader's, imagination. The arrangements for painless pleasure do not arouse in everyone the indignation they do in Bernard and the Savage. Yet these control characters, recalling both traditional morality and the romantic morality of intensity, establish some lacks in the scientific pleasure dome, and the reader can enjoy the suspect while officially occupying the highest ground.

Brave New World takes a great deal of its life from treating broadly the sexual conflict discovered in *Antic Hay*. The difference between maternal warmth, helpfulness, unworldliness and Mrs. Viveash's sexier, more egocentric temperament makes Gumbril play at love. He chooses, uneasily, the emancipated woman over the neo-Victorian. In *Brave New World* this conflict becomes central and somewhat disfiguring: the Savage, an esthetic mistake if a moral necessity, cannot resolve the difference between love as his mother has shown it and love as the Malthusian belt girls understand it. As Bernard resists but works at processing young people to society's values, the Savage resists but likes the new woman, freed from house and children, asserting her freedom to play.

Brave New World brings into the open Huxley's equivocal attitude toward change in manners and morals. Satire in the great Victorian novelists is normally progressive; its enemies hang on from the past—the Chancery Court in *Bleak House,* the idea of the gentleman in *Great Expectations,* the squirearchy in *Vanity Fair.* But twentieth century satire normally distrusts the future and finds value in remnants from the past—romantic intensity, the country family. The official morality in *Brave New World* opposes changes which are occurring, as Cary sees, because a great many people want them to.

What Huxley saw in the twenties and early thirties, then, was society organizing itself more and more for freedom through sexual play and rejecting older ideals of family affection and responsibility. What he foretold was simply more efficient organization for play. He did not foresee the succeeding decades' interest in power, stability, or career. Like his comedy, his satire remains a fairly comfortable view of catastrophe. But by the time Huxley had isolated the ideal of play enough to satirize it, a novelist far more involved with it and far less hopeful about primitive emotions had made it his own province.

CHAPTER FOUR

Stylized Rebellion

EVELYN WAUGH

MOST OF MY FRIENDS who like Evelyn Waugh act a little shamefaced about him, as though they were too old for such tricks and ought to be giving one more try to the Great Books. Their embarrassment persists even though history has vindicated them. Waugh is almost certainly the best British novelist of the depression decade—at worst, one of two or three who are read at all. He may be merely an entertainer with a style, but comedy is usually serious, however much some analysis may burlesque its kind of seriousness. Waugh's early novels have evocative power, and my friends' embarrassment suggests the presence of something they both like and prefer not to take to themselves.

But what? Primarily, I think, the narrowed view of reality and choice behind his memorable description of symptoms.

The symptoms appear as a virtuoso caricature of uncertainty and self-disgust trying to wear the face of assurance and vitality. Most of the heroes in his best comedies are unconfident confidence men. They are trying, in a contemporary and "American" way, to establish public personalities to evade their confusion about their own identities. Privately, they are unsure what they are, want, do not want, or can do next. So they by-pass the hard ways of gaining identity for the quick, brilliant impression. Their outrageous actions bring them some of the disapproving attention they need, but they both fear this drug and find it hard to get. They suffer not so much from the "fatal hunger for permanence" that Father Rothschild fears as from a fatal fear of indifference.

Even their efforts at gaining public confidence, though, depend on a public they ostensibly do not respect. In Waugh's latest novel, G. Pinfold suffers from hallucinatory voices (including one, Goneril, who suggests an unhappy identification with Lear). But these voices have always been in Waugh's novels—accusing, defending, promising, disregarding. Many, sometimes a majority, of the characters in the comic novels do nothing except talk about the main characters. Their voices are real, but they speak for the same guilt, doubt, and concern to impress as Pinfold's unreal voices—and Pinfold at least knows they are hallucinatory. The earlier characters need these commentators, heard and unheard, to give their effects resonance, and respond to their own echoes by trying to be what others say they are.

This crowd of observers, who take no interest in their own lives but only in the Bright Young People's, prove to Waugh and the main characters that nothingness has not yet caught up with them. Nevertheless, this audience, without meaning to offend, stirs up the flaw at the heart of the wish. The public never takes the rebels as they want to be taken, but comes just close enough to keep them trying harder than before. Worse, since they never quite believe in their public personalities, they see themselves as potentially "bogus"—their word foreshadowing Salinger's "phoney."

Beneath these symptoms, though, lies the view of reality and choice which is Waugh's most disturbing contribution. Childish exhibitionism is not, after all, everyone's problem; beats and Mayfair sets are always a minority expressing something that society as a whole feels drawn to, but does not care to express overtly. What Waugh writes is the sad history of all rebellions in manners, the slide from bold experiment to fashionable cliché.

The two postwar rebellions of this century have obvious similarities, but the important one is less obvious. In the ordinary view, idealistic young people horrified by slaughter and enforced conformity become angry and footloose. Edwardian adults were undoubtedly horrified by World War I, but Waugh was a child when it began—and children are more fascinated with toy machine guns than horrified by death. Huxley, Waugh, and Fitzgerald were not in the war, but saw older brothers and acquaintances go to war and leave them out of the excitement. Particularly in England, where the elite regiments maintain at least the formula that an aristocracy justifies itself by defending the nation and where regimental flags and histories have meant something, an aristocrat left out of a war is frustrated in his natural activity. (Waugh's second war experiences and novels show clearly this sense of a second chance.)

In any case, the rebellion arises not because a war begins, or continues, but because it ends. For all its front-line realities, war gives civilians a sense of an overriding common purpose, a kind of enforced, synthetic sense of community. It is frightening, exciting, chaotic, and full of opportunities. The war ends, but the taste for intensity and community has been inculcated in the rising generation and the noncombatants. Their rebellion is less a turning against the immediate past than an effort to carry it on under the unsuitable conditions of peace. Unfortunately, the forms of the rebellion must seem trivial and playful beside war itself or the war generation's attempt to recapture stability. Out of rather thin air the rebels try to invent the intensities of peace.

Literary histories usually pair Huxley and Waugh as a comedy team, but they actually represent two stages of the rebellion —Waugh comes half a generation later. Huxley's rebels in *Antic Hay* experiment with new attitudes and new ways of life based on the sense, which war also creates, that each individual must make his own pattern of life within the area of freedom he has. But Waugh's Bright Young People do not have *new* attitudes and they have no ideas. Instead they have fixed, even mandatory, ways of spending their time—working hard at "different" parties which turn out to be all the same. Their rebellion is not experimental, but fashionable.

Fashionable is a step, still highly self-conscious, toward traditional. (A few fashions in women's dresses become "classic.") The styles in talk, food, drink, activity, and outraging the elders have in Waugh become widespread, popular with at least an elite that takes pride in knowing the ropes. But in Huxley there are no ropes, only a group of fanatics trying to persuade each other that each has the right ethic and the right mode. Waugh shows the revolution in manners stabilized, popularized, flattened out. This stabilized revolution is his reality.

Since a fashionable rebellion by definition demands exhibition and publicity, it quickly creates its own dilemma: the experiments out of which it arose make harder and harder the invention of anything truly individual. In *Black Mischief,* a young married couple eat and drink in bed while entertaining their friends, some of them also in bed. Everyone treats the situation as perfectly normal. Sonia and Alastair are like that, this is their claim to attention, and convention requires that everybody respect everybody else's claim. Of course, Sonia and Alastair are playing to an unseen audience as well—office-going people, older people who if present would be scandalized. The next convolution requires the true rebel to outrage the merely fashionable rebels. So, before his conversion to "duty" in Azania, Basil Seal makes a point of appearing disheveled at fashionable parties to announce the end of a five-day "racket." With some of the girls, at least, this does give him the appearance of primitive strength. He thus deals with the threat of tameness, but not very imaginatively, and the greater threat of a failure of inventiveness hangs over the whole society.

By its nature Waugh's coterie cannot be a loose association of rebels like Huxley's, but grows tight and prescriptive. The coterie is doubtless an urban relative of the small town so necessary to regional American fiction, but in the city so many values and groups compete that no group can be sure that its order is *the* order. Whatever its advantages in getting publicity, the coterie must be insistent, even hysterical, in asserting its superiority. Moral stability means being in and knowing how to act there. The members of the coterie in *Vile Bodies* get great satisfaction from knowing that rich and important people like the prime minister's daughter want nothing more than to be just like them.

The situation creates its own set of fears—especially of being on the verge of being left out. The eighth Earl of Balcairn, a gossip columnist, commits suicide because exclusion ruins his livelihood. The world threat to the coterie is dissolution by natural processes—drifting away, marriage outside, geographical separation, new interests. For this process leaves the hard core of insiders outside.

My generalizations so far refer to the four significant novels written in the late twenties and early thirties—*Decline and Fall, Vile Bodies, Black Mischief,* and *A Handful of Dust.* I mean now to trace more concretely Waugh's evolution from testing fashionable rebellion by its internal weaknesses in *Vile Bodies* to accepting the logic of his view of human nature in society in *A Handful of Dust.* This logic, the narrowed view of reality and choice, runs like this: human beings are born into a world they never made and find it a conflict of styles; their only individuality consists in choosing the style suited to their backgrounds and temperaments. Thereafter they must live the choice to its logical outcome. The styles give in part what they promise, but no style can encompass the elemental demand to love and hate intensely.

(This view of reality and choice explains a great deal about why Waugh, antagonistically aristocratic, was nevertheless able to make his way as a novelist in the thirties. His approach to life is at heart sociological. The idea of choosing a party and fighting its battles has turned out to be a more fundamental aspect of the thirties' temper than the particular party chosen—witness Cozzens.)

Vile Bodies tests from the inside the ideals of fashionable rebellion. Its structure involves an accelerating race between gaiety and anxiety. The first six chapters establish the "normal" pattern of group life. Authority, represented by a customs official, arbitrarily cuts off Adam Symes' means of support by destroying the memoirs he has been writing. He establishes a home among the heavy drinkers at Lottie Crump's hotel, characteristically postponing the question of payment. The apparent action concerns his nonchalant, on-again, off-again marriage plans with Nina Blount, but Adam's real conflict comes from a desire to establish community with other people through new forms of gaiety—and a desire to escape the demands of this inhuman ideal. His courtship and presently his work come to the same thing, party-going, but actual emotions—disappointment, disgust, a wish for self-defeat—dilute the ideal emotions of fun and games. He creates continuing barriers to the marriage, most notably by giving a thousand pounds to a drunken major to put on a long-shot horse.

The memorable part of this first section suggests an anxiety which lies behind the desire for continual gaiety—the "faster and faster," as Agatha Runcible calls it. Though the characters conspire to hide their problems from themselves, Waugh shows, as a sort of ground fear, men afraid they are not masculine enough, women afraid that they are not feminine enough. The Hon. Agatha Runcible and the Hon. Miles Malpractice balance each other among the main characters, but an atmosphere of similar anxiety proceeds from Johnny Hoop, Mrs. Ape's angels, and a series of incidents.

The characters live with this problem, though, and accept it as ordinary. Their more painful conflicts arise from exhibitionism. Agatha Runcible, central character for this part of the novel, enjoys being stripped and searched by the customs matrons, and gets the story of the "outrage" on page one of all the papers. After an all-night party she finds herself in a grass skirt at the breakfast table at No. 10 Downing Street. ("A half-naked woman just ran into my study," the prime minister reports.) Confronted with the actual authority that her conduct is geared to shocking at second hand, she panics and rushes out into the street, to find the newspaper photographers waiting for her.

The early section sets up, too, the offensively understanding attitude of the older generation. Exhibitions that do not shock are half beaten from the start. Mr. Outrage, the Liberal prime minister who is now in and now out of office, plays the same game as the younger set—with a Japanese baroness. Lady Throbbing and Mrs. Blackwater, who date from Edwardian times, speak indulgently of the young people and wonder whether such antics are as much fun when open as when concealed. Colonel Blount, Nina's father, carries the strongest burden of the complaint. Adam and Nina hope, unrealistically, for his financial support during the first year of marriage, but Colonel Blount takes an interest only in the local movie house and the rector's automobile, and refuses to treat the young couple seriously as either a moral or a financial problem. He readily gives Adam a check for one thousand pounds, signed "Charlie Chaplin." Waugh's young people make a tremendous claim on their elders for example and support, and Colonel Blount provides only humorous indulgence without meaningful model or help.

In the second section of the novel responsibility falls on Adam for the most significant activity in his society—publicizing its doings—when he succeeds Lord Balcairn as gossip columnist. "Untamed youth," as the blurb puts it, can be sure of its existence only through the mirror of newspaper publicity. The gossip columnist sets up for his readers—and, more important, for the party-goers themselves—a myth of ideal gaiety which the party scenes constantly undercut. The participants cure their hangovers by reading what fun they really had. Adam adds to this natural mythologizing function by inventing archetypal characters who represent the ideals of the group. Ingenuity is the main quality of the parties, and he uses the same ingenuity to improve reality. He becomes the Basil Seal of London, happily sowing confusion by caricaturing ideals he considers himself past believing in. (The gossip columnist, incidentally, is a degraded version of the novelist who mythologizes an elite.)

But, though Waugh shows the gap between ideal and real for his elite, he is nevertheless of their party rather than of the pale group shown at Anchorage House. Some critics have seen Anchorage House as representing all that is solid and returnable to in English life. Actually, it is only another face of the absurd. Nina's distaste for sex undercuts the ideal of fun, but Lady Ursula's fright over her engagement to colorless Edward Throbbing caricatures the older ideal of duty. In Waugh a cheerful distaste for sex is better than a stuffy one. The presence of royalty at Anchorage House merely sanctions an absurd conspiracy.

The first section of the novel, then, shows the ordinary frenzied activities of the coterie, the second an effort to establish these as public values. In the final section the threat of emotional illness which has hung over the race against anxieties becomes actual and explicit. Agatha Runcible, who had meant to be only a chubby clown, becomes the pathetic heroine of the effort to down self-doubt by frenzy. In an atmosphere of drunken confusion, her badge of insiderdom—an arm band reading "Spare Driver"—

provides an opening for catastrophe. She replaces the injured driver, sets off drunkenly around the track, and crashes. In the nursing home, where she presently dies, she goes through a series of hallucinations about being back in the car—"faster and faster."

The strength of the novel comes from its inventive spirit and its contradictory anxieties. The ground fears about masculinity and femininity cannot be isolated from the others except artificially. There is the distaste for authority, ridiculed especially in government figures—and the desire for firm support from parents. Adam and Nina fear poverty and bill collectors, but Adam spends the whole novel trying to collect from the drunken major. The strongest fear, though, is of being taken in—by the major, by Colonel Blount, by publishers, by false fronts in government and society. Adam's own role multiplies this fear. He sees himself as a confidence man, making his way by a bold assertion of talents he may or may not have. Like Nina, he poses as a sophisticate in sex without much real experience. He takes the job as gossip columnist out of bravado and imposes casually on the credulity of his readers. He tries to charm Colonel Blount out of a thousand pounds and does get a thousand pounds betting with a stupid young man at the hotel. He gets spending money from the customers at the hotel by appealing boyishly to Lottie Crump. He naturally fears other confidence men.

The other great catchall fear is fear of failure. Its most obvious form is fear of, and desire for, failure in work. Adam worries that his inventiveness will fail. His fads antagonize his employer. He presently loses his job by failing to attend to it—because he has gone to get something for nothing out of Colonel Blount. He wavers between a wish to outrage taboos and a fear of retaliation. And anxiety about a failure of inventiveness runs through his whole set. After the party in a captive dirigible, there seems nothing left to do—until Miles Malpractice takes up auto racing. The group's cohesiveness depends upon finding new games, and how can anyone expect to go on inventing new ones?

"Oh, Nina, what a lot of parties."

(. . . Masked parties, Savage parties, Victorian parties, Greek parties, Wild West parties, Russian parties, Circus parties, parties where one had to dress as somebody else, almost naked parties in St. John's Wood, parties in flats and studios and houses and ships and hotels and night clubs, in windmills and swimming baths, tea parties at school where one ate muffins and meringues and tinned crab, parties at Oxford where one drank brown sherry and smoked Turkish cigarettes, dull dances in London and comic dances in Scotland and disgusting dances in Paris—all that succession and repetition of massed humanity . . . . Those vile bodies . . . .)

Vile Bodies celebrates a defeated ideal, which human nature cannot live up to or live without. The novel moves by precariously balancing opposites—a wish to impose by startling actions, a fear of discipline and disregard; a distaste for organized work, a hope of keeping ahead of the actual and emotional bill collectors.

One puzzling, undramatic character, the drunken major, wanders in and out, the unscathed carrier of the disease. He is a major—and the confidence man anonymous. He says that he put the money on the winning horse, promises immediate payment, brilliantly dodges making it, and ends as a general making love to Chastity, Mrs. Ape's fallen angel, on a battlefield. Waugh obviously likes and indulges him, primarily because he promises fulfillment of the unrealistic hopes for an easy way. He gets away with it all, as the main characters do not. He is a promise of resilience in tight spots; like Grimes in *Decline and Fall,* he demonstrates that nothing much can ever happen to an old public school man.

Readers familiar only with *Vile Bodies* may think of Waugh as the elegist of such elite coteries. Yet, mathematically at least, the majority of his good work shows a falling away from the coterie ideal. *Black Mischief* makes us distrust Waugh's sense of reality at the same time that he plays on a counterdistrust of our own. Without any program to give retreat a respectable air, he explores sympathetically the possibility of running away from anxiety and stalemate. Through all the mixed likes and dislikes of *Vile Bodies* and *Black Mischief,* he stays loyal to one quality— an odd naturalness. And for *natural* he reads *impulsive.* Anarchic, resistant impulse collides with society's prescriptions for work and pleasure, while the predatory enemies of impulse—

planning, literalness, orderliness, regulation—wait patiently outside the Embassy door for the rebel. Even Waugh's much-
publicized snobbishness is part of a more pervasive childhood
ideal of sport, support, and recognition without responsibility.
One appeal of the novels surely lies in their creating comedy
out of the painful mischances of this childhood ideal in a glamor-
ous adult milieu. Because his high society does not at first seem
entirely rule-bound, it offers a hope for elusive emotional freedom in an organizing world. Only an aristocrat in such a world
can be *natural,* can follow the dictates of impulse without severe
inhibition or consequence.

But impulsiveness can have a grimmer side, and Waugh knows
it. Little is usually said of the clearly-labeled regressions to primitive cultures in *Black Mischief* and *A Handful of Dust,* but
cheery naturalness can become angry confusion, and angry confusion creates its own demand for a vacation from reality. Basil
Seal is the first to embody this new Waugh conflict. The world
of "rackets," parties, and shifting love affairs is still his reality.
He lives in it and looks to it for his audience, but his mark of the
hero is that he does not really fit it. The prolonged periods of
drunkenness are more than a bid for attention; they are a symptom of dissatisfaction with the tameness of these society games.
For all their brightness and exhibitionism, the party-going
women like Angela and Basil's sister want harmless games,
though people are often accidentally hurt. Basil is a Huxley man
in a Waugh world, a real revolutionary spirit, he believes, among
stylized rebels. But he is a Huxley man minus the Obsession. He
merely "needs" a change from London and goes to Azania, an
African island, as the wildest change he can make.

In the best British tradition, though in no known British manner, Azania is the making of Basil. He is the prime representative of one Waugh pattern of action—the energy released by
doing something else when confronted by a clearly defined
"duty." As the son of a famous Conservative, he is expected to go
into politics, but, as a last resort, he goes on one of his "rackets"
and is arrested in the constituency carefully chosen to assure his
election. On the evening when he steals his mother's emeralds
and leaves for Azania, his elders are still visualizing him as a stu-

dent living on a tight allowance and becoming an important barrister.

But Azania means more to Basil than merely avoiding a family design for living. It means the opportunity to put in full time caricaturing the modern world's demand for action and especially for change in traditional, "natural" patterns. Seth, the Emperor of Azania, has been to Oxford and wants even more than London society to be fashionably modern—but Azania is never tame. Gallows stand outside the Palace offices for routine use in keeping up standards of housekeeping. Surreptitious garroting eliminates the losers in the continuing game of desertion during the equally continuous revolutions. Basil tells Prudence, the British minister's daughter, "I could eat you," and he does, literally—at a funeral feast of the Wanda tribesmen.

This casual, almost innocent, violence is only a symptom. Azania appeals most to Basil's sense that all directed human activity is absurd. The Emperor is the Huxley man Basil has been looking for—obsessive, active, and childlike. This grandson of a cannibal chief, who wants to Westernize his country in a One-Year Plan, has only the wildest, and most shifting, grasp of where to begin. Basil and Seth meet on the idea of making things really modern by destroying the traditional. Basil knows all the modes of action, but has never found any reason for using them. When Seth appoints him Minister of Modernization with extraordinary powers, he falls to with energy, the more so because almost all Seth's plans are destructive. The environment resists all constructive change, in any case, but shows genius for uproar and for the first time Basil feels his talents truly engaged.

Basil works so hard on Seth's plans for a "rational" ordering of the primitive society because he is confident the plans will fail and, even where they partly succeed, will work toward Sterility —one of Seth's slogans and, by Basil's estimate, the real value of London society. Seth's orders for one morning's work call for, among other improbabilities, abolishing infant mortality and tearing down the Anglican cathedral to build a boulevard. The main comedy of the novel follows from the natives' superb resistance to all planning. They celebrate the new birth control devices as fertility gods. The barefoot Imperial Guards eat their new boots at a special feast. To impress two women from the British S.P.C.A., the modernizers invite trouble by evicting the tough Earl of Ngumbo from his mansion and using it for a museum of Azanian culture. The Nestorian Patriarch organizes opposition to Sterility. Ultimately, the conservative forces overthrow Seth and drive Basil out of the country. Basil mourns Seth's death at the cannibal feast.

But it was all great fun while it lasted—earnest planning and furious energy in the name of sterility and destruction, the only forces capable of energizing Basil. The novel ends sadly with a joint protectorate restoring order, building one macadam road, and getting the trucks running, but with a staff of efficient, spiritless civil servants. Even the happy old lawn games and lost dispatches of the British Embassy have disappeared. The joyless adults have replaced the merry, dangerous children.

Black Mischief has been called snobbish about African natives; actually, Waugh is completely with them in their resistance to planning. Throughout the novel he allies the rational and the fashionable as artificial modes of channeling impulse, both absurd in the light of real human nature. The genuine state of man, which he must recognize and live with, is an angry confusion. Basil finds a happy angry confusion in Azania and Tony Last, in *A Handful of Dust,* a trapped, miserable one in Brazil, but they both deserve the reality they come to.

This conflict of genuine impulse and channelized action runs through Waugh's later work, even such extended jokes as *The Loved One*. On this issue Waugh is a saddened moralist. Some people, not the best, seem made to stylize their emotions within the rules—and they win all the prizes. Angry confusion always loses in the end. Brenda, Sir Humphrey Maltravers, Jock Grant-Menzies, Lady Metroland and their like win out. And the prizes are worth having. In the world of the fashionable and the reasonable, most women and some men are businesslike in pursuing the main chance. Waugh's later heroes do not believe there is a main chance until someone else has won it.

To this point Waugh's comic devices remain essentially the continuous inventions in *Decline and Fall*. They provide a guided tour through one country after another of absurdity. The reader comes in turn upon Dr. Fagan, Prendergast, Captain Grimes, Lady Metroland, and Dr. Silenus or upon Agatha Runcible, the drunken major, and Colonel Blount. Events like the school games, the party in the captive dirigible, and the S.P.C.A. ladies' visit dominate. No one situation or character appears long enough to risk boring anyone, though in each succeeding novel the area of maneuver becomes tighter. In the first two novels the relatively neutral heroes act as both protagonists and guides. In *Black Mischief*, however, the hero does not take his aims out of the air around him, but begins to rebel against them and look for his own way, and in *A Handful of Dust* the hero has solidified in his own way.

A highly concrete style for showing absurdity does most to hold the early novels together. Unlike Huxley's characters, who take their tone largely from their main stance, Waugh's cultivate their oddities and mix them through their whole lives. New details evolve with every reappearance. Minor characters often become comic by a density of detail only slightly exaggerated:

> [Professor Silenus] was not yet very famous anywhere, though all who met him carried away deep and diverse impressions of his genius. He had first attracted Mrs. Beste-Chetwynde's attention with the rejected design for a chewing-gum factory which had been reproduced in a progressive Hungarian quarterly. His only other completed work was the decor for a cinema film of great length and complexity of plot—a complexity rendered the more inextricable by the producer's austere elimination of all human characters, a fact which had proved fatal to its commercial success. He was starving resignedly in a bed-sitting room in Bloomsbury, despite the untiring efforts of his parents to find him—they were very rich in Hamburg—when he was offered the commission of rebuilding King's Thursday. "Something clean and square"—he pondered for three hungry days upon the aesthetic implications of these instructions and then began his designs.
>
> "The problem of architecture, as I see it," he told a journalist who had come to report on the progress of his surprising creation of ferro concrete and aluminum, "is the problem of all art—the elimination of the human element from the consideration of form. The only perfect building must be the factory, because that is built to house machines, not men."

Colonel Blount, however, is comic not merely because he is himself an unchartable eccentric, but because Adam comes expecting a stereotype father and finds the Colonel. And in *A Handful of Dust,* the main characters do not so much produce comedy in their own right as become comic by juxtaposition.

In *Black Mischief* Basil Seal leaves the coterie, but retains his membership and returns in the last chapter. His trip to Azania is a vacation from all that. *A Handful of Dust* tests a new and more desperate answer. Suppose a man could assert the actualities of his temperament and yet find a style reasonably consistent with it; would he not have solved the conflict? Only, as the novel works out, if the style is the current one or he can sacrifice all involvement with his contemporaries.

In the early novels Waugh worries the realities of inhibition and self-discipline while trying to escape them; in *A Handful of Dust* he comes round at last to viewing them as human and even sympathetic qualities. Basil Seal is too enthusiastic for the coterie; Tony Last is too unenthusiastic. But he is nevertheless another rebel against the women's world of orthodox unorthodoxy, of fashionable décor and affairs. Tony knows himself by his negations. He does not like people much and never in large groups. He chooses the Victorian role of responsible country gentleman after the culture has ceased to support it and for a time involves his pretty wife Brenda in the game. Tony takes pride in their "bad" Victorian house, plans for more bathrooms, sits on rural committees, plays squire to the villagers at church, and even sponsors a fox hunt, although he does not like killing animals. Brilliant incidental sketches like the old vicar's sermons, developed during long service in India, reinforce the anachronism. ("The Reverend Tendril 'e do speak uncommon high of the Queen," a gardener's wife once remarked to Tony.) The main tension, and bitter comedy, derives from Brenda's extended leaving. In taking an apartment in London and hiring an unsuccessful gigolo, she wants both fun and her old position—another vacation from a style too tame for her. She holds Tony at arms' length and soothes him just enough to keep up his hopes. The situation could have become a study in masochism, and something of the sort may account for Waugh's interest, but he manages his sympathies skillfully. He tells this part of the novel from Brenda's point of view, so that her cruelty to Tony seems only what she thinks it is—a harmless wish, indulged by all her friends, for sport and freedom. The heart of her new high culture is the prescribed talk—self-consciously egocentric—which evaluates novelties and, even more, denies the traditional obligations of love and family. At her sister's in London, before Beaver has even telephoned her, she has the language perfectly:

> Brenda had come into Marjorie's room and they were having breakfast in bed. Marjorie was more than ever like an elder sister that morning. "But really, Brenda, he's such a *dreary* young man."
>
> "I know it all. He's second rate and a snob and, I should think, as cold as a fish, but I happen to have a fancy for him, that's all. . . . He got engaged once but they couldn't get married because of money and since then he's never had a proper affair with anyone decent . . . he's got to be taught a whole lot of things. That's part of his attraction."

When the gossip starts before the affair has started, Brenda has an answer:

> "So Polly's on to your story. She'll be telling everyone in London at this moment."
>
> "How I wish there was anything to tell. The cub hasn't even rung me up. . . . Well, I'll leave him in peace. If he doesn't do anything about me, I'll go down to Hetton this afternoon. Perhaps that's him." But it was only Allan from the Conservative Central office, to say how sorry he had been not to get to the party the night before. "I heard Brenda disgraced herself," he said.
>
> "Goodness," said Brenda. "People do think that young men are easily come by."

She shows some concern for Tony's comfort, and tries to provide him a mistress, but, when he continues to be a "stick," puts him off with such skill that the reader becomes involved in the game of deception and withdrawal, the old Waugh confidence game. The telephone becomes the symbol of her inaccessibility. Tony's slow recognition of the facts makes his calls during a night club bout both comic and pathetic.

Edmund Wilson has said that Waugh alone of his generation can create lovable women. Brenda would not strike everyone as lovable, but she certainly has resilience, emotional invulnerability most of the time, and "winning ways." Her vitality comes through in her confidence that Tony will, and should, indulge her against his own interests, and in her sureness of what she wants to do and how to do it. (Tony only knows what he does not want to do.) She accepts Polly Cockpurse, who has slept her way into society, and Mrs. Beaver, the commercial spirit behind the fashionable ladies' chic, as her guides. Tony is Brenda's dupe, but Brenda is Polly Cockpurse's and Mrs. Beaver's. She leaves Tony partly because she wants to boss and instruct John Beaver, and becomes the dupe of people who live by exploiting fashionable rebellion.

In the early stages Brenda is a tease, wanting indulgence and freedom without quite leaving home. The painful comedy plays on Tony's trying to act as if nothing had changed, and reaches its height when their son, John Andrew, dies in a hunting accident. Waugh plays Tony's concern for Brenda's feelings against the succeeding scene where she hears the news. (Her gigolo is also named John, but not John Andrew.)

> "What is it, Jock? Tell me quickly, I'm scared. It's nothing awful is it?"
>
> "I'm afraid it is. There's been a very serious accident."
>
> "John?"
>
> "Yes."
>
> "Dead?"
>
> He nodded.
>
> She sat down on a hard little Empire chair against the wall, perfectly still with her hands folded in her lap, like a small well-brought-up child introduced into a room full of grown-ups. She said, "Tell me what happened? Why do you know about it first?"
>
> "I've been down at Hetton since the week end."
>
> "Hetton?"
>
> "Don't you remember? John was going hunting today."
>
> She frowned, not at once taking in what he was saying. "John . . . John Andrew . . . I . . . Oh thank God . . . " Then she burst into tears.

Brenda has not become hard-boiled through harsh experiences. Mrs. Slattery, who has done just that, shows unusual human sympathy during the hours after John Andrew's death, but Brenda merely puts play above every tie. After the accident she shows as much disinclination as Waugh himself to talk the matter over and get to the heart of her dissatisfaction with Tony. The dissatisfaction itself is the heart of the matter for her. Fashionable change is her métier, as outdated routine is Tony's. Her final concern with her old home sets Mrs. Beaver redecorating a bedroom in chrome plate.

Tony's devotion to the role of country gentleman can easily be exaggerated. In it he is doing his duty, fitting into an established style, but his real talent is for resisting Brenda's modern world. He genuinely dislikes the activities and people she likes. He hates week-end visitors, though he dutifully bores them all by guided tours of the house. He hates Brenda's London friends, especially Mrs. Beaver, with her fashionable dress shop, fashionable bedrooms, and fashionable gossip. The careless talk of these women among themselves supports his distaste.

The incidental characters reinforce the comedy of breakdown in communication. The mistress whom Brenda and her friends choose for Tony, Jenny Abdul Akbar, is the divorced wife of a Moroccan prince who, by her account, did unspeakable things to her. Juxtaposing this "good trier" and the gentleman too polite to express himself emphasizes the distance between London and Hetton:

> "I expect you'd like to see your room," said Tony. "They'll bring tea soon."
>
> "No, I'll stay here [said Jenny]. I like just to curl up like a cat in front of the fire, and if you're nice to me I'll purr, and if you're cruel I shall pretend not to notice—just like a cat . . . Shall I purr, Teddy?"
>
> "Er . . . yes . . . do, please, if that's what you like doing."
>
> "Englishmen are so gentle and considerate. It's wonderful to be back among them . . . mine own people. Sometimes when I look back at my life, especially at times like this among lovely old English things and kind people, I think the whole thing must be a frightful nightmare . . . then I remember my *scars*. . . ."
>
> "Brenda tells me you've taken one of the flats in the same house as hers. They must be very convenient."

"How English you are, Teddy—so shy of talking about personal things, intimate things . . . I like you for that, you know. I love everything that's solid and homely and *good* after . . . after all I've been through."

"You're not studying economics too, are you, like Brenda?"

"No; is Brenda? She never told me. What a wonderful person she is. When *does* she find the time?"

"Ah, here comes tea at last," said Tony. "I hope you allow yourself to eat muffins. So many of our guests nowadays are on a diet. I think muffins one of the few things that make the English winter endurable."

"Muffins stand for so much," said Jenny.

Midway through the novel Waugh shifts suddenly to Tony's point of view and the tone changes. Waugh treats Tony's rebellion, when he finally rebels, as an understandable, even justified, but clear-cut regression. After a grotesque failure to do the "right thing" in an arranged adultery, Tony refuses Brenda's demand for a large financial settlement and embarks on the Waugh search for identity by regression to a primitive, though still social, world. But his exploration of the upper Amazon merely makes real the feeling of desertion and isolation which he already has. The later scenes, some of Waugh's most imaginative, caricature Tony's effort to establish a clearing of anachronistic order in a wilderness of angry confusion. He is looking for a mythical lost city of Victorian Gothic, but the Indian porters desert, the leader of the expedition drowns, and Tony, seriously ill with malaria, troubled by hallucinations of reconciliation with Brenda, is barely rescued. Mr. Todd, his rescuer, is as madly unmodern as the Emperor Seth is madly modern. Tony, believed dead in England, ends as a prisoner in the jungle reading the collected works of Dickens to his demented rescuer. Tony finds his role—lost, imprisoned, mewed up with the great Victorians—but it is the role he has to play rather than one he, or anyone, would have chosen.

But, given time, Brenda's way works. Her gigolo deserts when the settlement falls through, she feels poor and depressed for a while, then marries an old friend of Tony's, a member of the gay set become Conservative M. P. This success obviously fascinates

Waugh. The women's world of stylized rebellion has all the prizes and titles—earls, M. P.'s, home secretaries, the powerful and prestigious of the man's world. These men do not do the world's work very well—Jock's speech on the Pig Question is scarcely well-informed—and the women do not provide the fun they promise. But between the two groups a working arrangement exists and controls. The problem of unmerited success bothers Waugh because, in another fashion, it is his ideal.

Waugh's most famous satire, *The Loved One,* bears more angrily on some of the conflicts in the comic novels. The opening— slightly debased Graham Greene or early Conrad—seems to place the action in Waugh's primitive world:

> All day the heat had been barely supportable but at evening a breeze arose in the West, blowing from the heart of the setting sun and from the ocean, which lay unseen, unheard behind the scrubby foothills. It shook the rusty fringes of palm-leaf and swelled the dry sounds of summer, the frog-voices, the grating cicadas, and the ever present pulse of music from the neighboring native huts.
>
> In that kindly light the stained and blistered paint of the bungalow and the plot of weeds between the veranda and the dry waterhole lost their extreme shabbiness, and the two Englishmen, each with his whiskey and soda and his outdated magazine. . . .

But, for all this distance and scorn, Hollywood is really another version of the chromium world. Dennis complains, like Basil and Tony, that the style has overwhelmed the individual.

> American mothers, Dennis reflected, presumably knew their daughters apart, as the Chinese were said subtly to distinguish one from another of their seemingly uniform race, but to the European eye the Mortuary Hostess was one with all her sisters of the air-liners and the reception desks, one with Miss Poski at the Happier Hunting Ground.

But Hollywood's special claim in the chromium world is its *speed* in changing styles. Baby Aaronson becomes Juanita del Pablo and then an Irish colleen as the Spanish Civil War and the Legion of Decency in turn dominate the producers' consciousness.

Some American critics have taken Waugh's satire as a Catholic versus secular view of death. The Catholic novelist wants to face death morbidly; the secular world wants to console the survivors. And what is so wrong about that? But in those terms even Waugh might be able to answer, Nothing. Hollywood becomes the Enemy because it has developed a system for smothering angry confusion, the ultimate sense of identity in Waugh. The deaths in *The Loved One* are not just death in general; Sir Francis and Aimée commit suicide. Sir Francis, the belles-lettrist of an earlier day condemned to seeing literary fashions outmode him, has adapted to change after change, declining slowly from script writing into publicity. "I was always the most defatigable of hacks." But when he fails to adapt to one more change and the bosses remove his office furniture without notice, he hangs himself, freezing on his face the angry horror he means to convey.

But the art of Mr. Joyboy and Aimée can smother even this protest against the heartless style:

> "We had a Loved One last month who was found drowned. He had been in the sea a month and they only identified him by his wrist-watch. They fixed that stiff," said the hostess, disconcertingly lapsing from the high diction she had hitherto employed, "so he looked like it was his wedding day. The boys up there sure know their job. Why if he'd sat on an atom bomb, they'd make him presentable."

Mr. Joyboy's art, heightened by love, presents the indefatigable hack's corpse in the Radiant Childhood smile. "All for you, Miss Thanatogenos," and he has erased Sir Francis' final rebellion.

The rest of the novel, with superb satire on the techniques of smothering, deals in revenge. The satirical high point exploits Yeats' death-wish poem in the Lake Isle of Innisfree, where the dynamo makes sure that bees murmur continuously. But the revenge against Mr. Joyboy through Aimée is so serious that its handling all but loses Dennis the reader's confidence. The reconstructers adapt each corpse to a prefabricated style. In the same way Aimée proves unable to recognize Dennis as an individual poet. The classics which he provides as his own all sound alike. When she chooses Mr. Joyboy's more plastic art, Dennis drives her into the confusion that leads to her suicide, and revenges himself against the whole smothering process by erasing her, without style, in the incinerator at Happy Hunting Ground.

A recent English critic regrets that nobody nowadays writes social comedy like *Vile Bodies, Black Mischief,* and *A Handful of
Dust.* Nobody can, least of all Waugh. The culture and a writer's
own emotional development are too closely intertwined. Some
critics have suggested that Catholicism ruined him as a writer;
the argument that it made him is equally plausible. His faith in a
Catholic nobility in *Brideshead Revisited* merely records his loss
of faith in the youthful conflicts that had made him significant.
He was a Catholic when all the novels discussed were written.
Possibly because of his need for detachment, his work has always
shown an odd time lag. He wrote his school novel, *Decline and
Fall,* in the year of his marriage, 1928; his courtship novel in the
year of his divorce and conversion, 1930; his divorce novel four
years later; and his religious novel two years later still.

Waugh's best novels record the rise and fall of faith in a mixture of inhibition and impulse, a happy, anxious, finally angry
confusion. His characters do not work through their problems,
even tragically, but compound their confusion. *Decline and
Fall* shows a tentative sortie into high life and a withdrawal
after finding it too tricky. *Vile Bodies* deals with acceptance and
participation in a rebel elite which undermines itself. *Black
Mischief* shows an exploratory vacation from a rebellion become stylized, and *A Handful of Dust* faces the impossibility of
even embarking on such a rebellion. His characteristic conflict
evolves from the power of stylized rebellion to shape the lives of
people too sensitive or too hostile to live by its code.

The times and a writer's emotional progess may be worse for
him than for his readers. Nobody can write social comedy like
Jane Austen nowadays either. Waugh's fashionable rebellion has
its high moments, and has established itself. Little as Waugh resembles Forster, his sympathetic characters too struggle toward
community of spirit and, for a time, achieve it. For the rest, his
good novels remain a series of brilliant disturbances which call
back, cheerily and painfully, the reckless wishes we have resigned, overlaid, recognized, controlled, but never quite put to
sleep. We are a little shamefaced in reading him because, like his
heroes, we protect our hopes that we are beyond all that.

CHAPTER FIVE

Paradoxes of Pleasure-and-Pain

HENRY GREEN

HENRY GREEN published his first novel, *Blindness*, two years before Waugh's *Decline and Fall*. But, while Waugh was succeeding quickly, Green was working slowly toward the most important innovations in the comic novel since Joyce.

Most readers of Green like him for extraordinarily funny scenes like Edie's telling Kate she has found the Captain in Mrs. Jack's bed or old Rock angrily waiting for his breakfast handout in the girls' school kitchen. But many readers finish *Loving* or *Concluding*, as I did, unsure of what else happened. There is something to be said for leaving the situation at that. Scenes are obviously Green's natural units and it is easy to suspect that, if the general direction were only a little clearer, we might not like it anyway. Still, the effort to say more accurately what we have read tells us something not only about him and ourselves, but also something of what we really think—or suspect—about his predecessors.

Green is the skilled novelist in an age which does not want to look very far backward or very far forward—a war generation that lumps all the precariousness of human destiny under fear of the bomb and that lives with so great a social and physical mobility as to make ideals of continuity and traditional living like Forster's seem impossible. Green inherits and absorbs Joyce's use of modern psychology, though he transfers Joyce's view of the mind from the world of reflection to the world of behavior. Like Joyce—and Freud—he treats the mind as a symbol-making agent ready to assimilate every object and experience to its main obsessions. But Joyce had to document his view partly because neither he nor his readers could accept his "forging anew the conscience of the race" without proof. Green assumes this conscience *and* assumes that his readers will assume it—seems, in fact, unable to conceive any other way of thinking. So his most visible talent is for a casual and cheery acceptance of the human nature which Joyce had to prove and Lawrence became prophetic about.

But, though Green skims the sauce and vegetables off the depth psychology casserole, he does not take much meat. He is sensitive, often oversensitive to symbols, but his comic characters have no history. Their pasts, if any—most have none at all—are backdrops rather than moral evolutions. They live in the immediate future. Their internal monologues, if they had them, would probably run: here I am, here is what I am, here is what I want or have to do, how can I do it and like it? His characters allow for their own inadequacies and for a sort of microcosmic absurdity, but do not ask who they are or how they came here. So his scenes are always hurrying toward the next few minutes or the next few days, and carry little of the history which Joyce implies and Warren treats as the foundations of identity.

Green's psychological subtleties are of another kind, a twist on the turn which Huxley and Waugh in their early work gave to the comic novel. The comic novel from Meredith to Forster had a basis in truth to nature—a morally earnest effort toward accommodation between human nature and dominant forces in the culture. Huxley and Waugh focus the moral issue on an almost frantic search for enjoyment, heightened by outraging convention, and end their novels on the exhaustion that follows the frenzy. But, for Green, continuing conflict rather than struggle-and-resolution is the pattern of experience. The "war against the grown-ups" can be only an element, for he sees that we are both the children and the grown-ups. To change a little Forster's well-known phrase about "the knowledge of good-and-evil," Green treats not play and pain but play-and-pain. He sees experience as an hour-to-hour, day-to-day shift in the ratio of pleasure and pain, and cares far less than Huxley or Waugh about the major cycles. In a Green novel, action goes along with a mixture of wishes and fears, neither a direct forecast of the future. What does not happen is as important as what does happen—more important to defining the nature of anxiety. *Loving* sets a problem of wishes and anxieties, with a partial fulfillment of the wishes and strong desires to flee from the anxieties. *Concluding* presents the problem of living with wishes and actual phobias, but the characters do live with their phobias and do get some of their wishes.

Like many recent novelists, Green is a miniaturist with an angle. He deals with the conflict between the neurotic and the vital in personality and, by extension, between neurotic and lively people. His talent for casual and cheery acceptance of this situation is as much a matter of temperament as of understanding. He is good at *loving* what people find difficult to accept in themselves and their friends. He has, like Sterne, an extraordinary ability to like eccentrics and individualists, and to live cheerily with human weakness. He shares with many modern novelists a capacity for getting around conscience in the older sense—accepts easily, for example, a pervasive sexuality in the daily round of his characters. He likes the shrewdness by which handicapped, irregular characters get along in an organized, regularizing world, admires their capacity for giving some order to anxieties which threaten to become chaotic. He specializes in people trying to get what they want when appetites are weak and resistance strong.

But he emphasizes capable neurotics. He respects action that deals with problems as they come up, and satirizes passivity and awkwardness. His passive characters regularly get the leftovers. His *bête noir* is young Albert in *Loving*—the gawky, ashamed youth who does nothing in situations that require doing something, then takes "heroic" action to compensate. His favorite adjective, and adverb, is "sharp"—one character quickly taking up another's aggression before it gets under way and dealing summarily with it. And he has the contemporary ambivalent attitude toward organization and institutions. He admires efficient people who can handle other people and organize solutions to problems, but the organizations they create are constantly cramping the organizers as well as the cranky, eccentric, vigorous individualists.

His struggles of the sexes have the same friendly feeling for the contradictory. He caricatures the moral and temporal authority of mothers and substitute mothers—Miss Burch, Nanny Swift, Mrs. Welch, and Mrs. Tennant in *Loving* alone—yet his heroines are potentially maternal young—and sometimes not young—women. He treats the transition from teasing, flirtatious love to planning, semi-maternal, married relations. He is superb at showing dogged devotion to "small" personal concerns in a world of "large" events which seem to be passing the principals by and engaging their interest only as by-products of their personal problems. He uses the reverse stereotype of the uncertain man and the confident, competent woman, but adds bluster as one mark of this doubting masculinity and nagging as its feminine equivalent. He shows a continuing conflict between the wish for the maternal in woman and the wish to maintain individuality and bachelorhood against organizing, marrying women. His men are not sexually aggressive, his women alternately tease and sympathize—a combination that worries and pleases him. His individualism combines with a strong feeling for groups, especially groups with more women than men.

Though he writes another kind of novel almost as well, the general view of *Loving* as Green's best novel is accurate. The demand for some explanation of its structure is more than academic. There is just enough order, disrupted constantly by farce, to make the reader feel that he missed something which would explain the whole. The plot is not the difficulty. A group of servants keep things going in an Irish castle which gives them a refuge from the war, two of them fall in love and run away to England to be married. And, plainly, there is the fairy tale framework, which begins

> Once upon a day an old butler called Eldon lay dying in his room attended by the head housemaid, Miss Agatha Burch . . . .
> One name he uttered over and over, "Ellen."

and returns to this unseen Ellen two paragraphs before the end:

> "Edie," he [Raunce] appealed soft, probably not daring to move or speak too sharp for fear he might disturb her. Yet he used exactly that tone Mr. Eldon had employed at the last when calling his Ellen. "Edie," he moaned.

And the final sentences say

> The next day Raunce and Edith left without a word of warning. Over in England they were married and lived happily ever after.

But what happened between? Does the novel have a structure obscured by the short, shifting scenes or is its apparently reckless picking up of everything its principle of movement?

An honest answer would be *yes* to both questions. The novel does have a structure and one of its elements is the carrying on that ignores all anxieties and obstacles. But the basis of Green's skill is the free rolling interplay between his symbols and his characters' minds. (He sometimes seems obscure because a multitude of symbols float so loosely in the novel that the key ones are lost. And every important symbol has at least two meanings—a general, often sexual one which reflects human nature and a personal one which each character attaches to the object or experience.) Most of the characters in *Loving* are more easily worried by symbols than by events—they have established methods for dealing with events. Edith, the beautiful, lively housemaid, is not afraid to "find" Mrs. Tennant's ring because the possible penalty does not seem real to her. She learns about findings from Raunce, the butler, and makes no distinction between large and small ones. But she goes outside around the castle rather than go through the deserted rooms, and considers it proof of Raunce's masculinity that he looks for her by going through the rooms with sheet-covered furniture. Mrs. Jack endures a long scene of symbolic double talk with her mother-in-law in the "dairy" drawing room where almost every sentence of Mrs. Tennant's and even every object she picks up suggests to Mrs. Jack suspicion about her affair with Captain Davenport. In the picnic scene, Edith's manipulation of the scarf with "I love you, I love you" written all over it teases young Albert as much as anything she says or does. There are many episodes like Raunce's showing Edith the mouse caught in the dumb-waiter and the passing of the dead, moulding peacock, which no one wants to get caught with, to Mrs. Welch's larder and on to Albert's boiler. And when apprehensions grow about the lost ring, Miss Burch, the stiff Victorian housekeeper, demands that the drains be dug out again —a point she has already carried before. Most of the mix-ups and anxieties in the novel come because someone, most often everyone, has appropriated an object or act to his own obsession.

If this is the mode of Green's comedy in *Loving*, its theme is "free" love and responsibility. The structural symbol is the lost ring. Mrs. Tennant considers the loss a nuisance. She loses objects of value regularly, but this time the consequences disturb the security she wants from ownership of the castle. The insurance company investigates and refuses to insure further. Mrs. Tennant's loss of the ring implies loss of direction and loss of capacity for loving, while its passing to Edith, who has both in plenty, is the passing of a symbol of power. The consequence for Mrs. Tennant is anxiety. There is a thief in the castle, the servants are conspiring to keep things from her as well as take things from her, and Mrs. Jack is hiding some secret about Captain Davenport.

But the ring is more important to the servants, in whom Green's two aspects of reality, love and work, come together. Before Mrs. Tennant loses the ring, the main action is Charley's establishing himself as Raunce, the butler, rather than Charley the footman or "Arthur," the generic name Mrs. Tennant uses for all unimportant male servants. To do this he has to bluff his way past Miss Burch, who resists out of devotion to the dead Mr. Eldon, a dislike for change, and a well-grounded distrust of Raunce. Simultaneously, the action develops an especially cheery brand of pansexual loving. Raunce is coming to like Edith, but he chases both of the maids and can kiss Kate with energy. Kate and Edie are still living in the good old days of long talks about boy friends accompanied by gigglings, undressings, and back rubbings. Raunce bullies and defends young Albert. Miss Burch is devoted to her maids and tries hard to protect them from "dangers"—Raunce's attentions and finding Mrs. Jack in bed with the

Captain. (They are, of course, a good deal more capable than Miss Burch of dealing with both.) All the potential guardians of the moral law are happily ineffective. Mrs. Tennant is too unconcerned, Miss Burch is too horrified by events, and old Nanny Swift, sick, believes only good and sees no evil, hears no evil. The results are merrily anarchic.

But this anarchy has its efficient side. Raunce performs his duties as butler—mostly by ordering Albert to do them. Miss Burch supervises, Kate and Edie work hard, Edie brings Raunce his tea in bed before breakfast, and Albert does almost everything else. Mrs. Welch drinks but cooks, and is sensitive about the product.

Through all this Edie becomes so attractive and vital that some critics have called her the central character. But her very naturalness and energy make it impossible for her to be the main dramatic figure. She has no inner conflict and very little outer, though other girls might have a good deal over taking Raunce for a husband. Her flirtatious and accepting spirit creates problems for others, Raunce especially, but she herself is a force-of-nature character, one of the many in literature who lead others on to a more mixed experience. She knows instinctively how to live, Raunce must always figure out how to do it. Edie is a child of nature modified by the traditions of "service." Raunce has strong inner and outer conflicts that make for drama.

The loss of the ring appears at first to be only another episode, almost predictable, in this cheerful anarchy. Edith finds it and becomes engaged to Raunce at almost the same time. But the ring is an engagement ring in the existentialist sense, too. Mrs. Tennant leaves, apparently freeing the servants to do as they please. From that point on, for Raunce, the cheeriness, the effort to get established, and the free loving begin to give way to anxiety, the trials of responsible position, and possessiveness over Edith. Just as he has persuaded Miss Burch to recognize him as butler, the situation threatens to get beyond his control. He prides himself upon his craft and suavity. (He has set up a small system of cheating on the books weekly, though he has found no way to tap the profitable blackmail his predecessor had built up from Captain Davenport.) More than anything else, he wants a smooth-running organization. But, though he has the script for this operation in mind, he constantly meets absurd situations which interrupt his plans and force him to readjust. For Raunce, as for more serious characters, the absurd is the unexpected, irrational turn of events and emotions which deviate from his prepared script. The test of Raunce's competence is his ability to withstand these small jars. When he finds that Edith means to keep the ring as a nest egg for their marriage, he has to explain practical morality to her without losing her love. Edith traps him into admitting the amount of his weekly findings, but his habitual caution makes him try to downgrade the estimate within a day or two. When Edith's weakness for children leads to their theft of the ring from her, Raunce has to concoct a new plan which involves, to his taste, trusting too many people. Just as he has readjusted to this perspective, the lisping insurance investigator, ridiculous but threatening—a prime symbol of the difficulties in *Loving*—appears to cross-question the servants. Young Albert, out of a misplaced feeling that Edith needs protecting, "confesses" to the crime. Raunce blusters his way through this situation, but with a loss of poise and with the investigator's threat not to pay the claim increasing the threat in Mrs. Tennant's return.

The investigator's card, with its initials I.R.A. (Irish Regina Assurance), sets off a new round of the general wartime apprehensions into which the lesser characters translate their personal anxieties. Raunce has been using the threat of war service for women in England, along with the invasion talk, to keep Kate from going back home, but now he has to deal with semi-hysterical fears which have hitherto been peripheral—the I.R.A. (Irish Republican Army) is going to attack the castle, the Germans are going to invade Ireland as a steppingstone to England and rape all the women (old Miss Burch toys with this idea), the Irishman Paddy is a secret I.R.A. man who is going to betray them. But all the worries, real and imaginary, are mixed in with the also half-hysterical horseplay about the investigator's lisp.

The ring, the investigation, and the threat of further investiga-

tion aggravate Raunce's anxieties about marriage.* He begins
to turn up unexpectedly while Edith is teasing young Albert or
doing Captain Jack's room, and to question her about possible
advances from Captain Jack. Raunce's script for living calls for
smooth progress of his limited plans plus being "properly val-
ued." The events which interfere make no sense, and his anxiety
that he cannot deal with them increases along with his anxiety
about the engagement to Edie. His symptoms increase, too—his
glands become enlarged and he has to wear a neckcloth, his fear
of being outside the castle in the open air reasserts itself in spite
of Edith's coaxings. When his mother refuses to help him establish a family by moving to Ireland and Mrs. Tennant refuses to
value him properly, he slips out of Ireland with Edie and returns
to war work and his mother in England—a compromise with the
typical Raunce dubiousness about it. He goes into the marriage
hesitantly yet insistently, and he gives up trying to manage either Edith or the castle. The desire to do as he is told and let
someone else manage seems to triumph, yet to the end of the
novel he is busy managing the clandestine trip. He accepts his
public responsibility in wartime England, but by running away
from the more immediate responsibility which has become too
complex—as young Albert runs away from his inadequacies to
become a hero as a tail gunner.

Loving is the showpiece of one symbolic action Green has repeated in all his comic works—*Living, Party-Going, Nothing,
Doting,* even *Concluding.* From his first novel onward he has
been trying to prove that people who, by some going standard,
ought not to be enjoying life are enjoying it and that other people who ought to be enjoying it are not. Paradoxes on the con-
ventions of pleasure are his specialties. But he cannot give over
the problem, as Huxley and Waugh do in their comic novels, by
showing that the human animal is not made for enjoyment. He
wants too much to find the unexpected pleasure amid anxiety,
exasperation, pain, moral stasis.

His most persistent formula for resolving the paradox is "easy

* Earle Labor's "Henry Green's Web of Loving," *Critique,* IV (Fall-Winter,
1961), gives a thorough account of the threatening elements in the courtship
and marriage.

does it." His people who conscientiously try to have fun, like his people who try to do good, never do. The playboys and playgirls in *Party-Going*, Mrs. Jack in *Loving*, and the Middletons in *Doting* all fail by trying too hard too directly. But his factory workers in *Living*, the servants in *Loving*, the retired playboy and playgirl in *Nothing*, the retired scientist who slops pigs in *Concluding*, and the bachelor and plain secretary in *Doting* have fun by dealing with the immediate without expecting too much. They work on limited but possible goals and refuse to concentrate on some total, permanent good. Green works with dynamic rather than static concepts of enjoyment. The truly unhappy people in his novels want to organize life too thoroughly and, while Green likes the organizers for enjoyment better than the organizers for public good, he sees an obsessiveness common to both groups.

But here, too, Green lives on contradictions. In spite of this distaste for organization and drive, no novelist admires more than Green small schemes and smooth-working organization— but he wants the schemes to be petty and the organizations small and loose. He loves the ins and outs of the urgency that he dislikes. His "easy does it" takes hold because he recognizes the force of the driving spirit. He plays the urge to drive immediately toward the best against the necessity of indirection and limited aims.

Many people undoubtedly think of Green as a purely comic novelist, but long sections of *Party-Going, Caught,* and *Back* make unpleasant reading because of his preoccupation with depression. *Caught* and *Back* explore depression almost as far as the later novels of Anthony Powell. In the best comic novels Green hits an equilibrium between this depression and his extraordinarily cheery ability to accept human nature. But one of his best novels, *Concluding*, pegs the equilibrium so far on the side of dread that there is a question whether it is comic at all.

Concluding is certainly about the deeper, more unresolvable anxieties. In spite of all the worries, *Loving* treats only two real grounds for anxiety—Raunce's inadequacy as butler-manager and the complications in his love for Edith. But the dread which hangs over the characters in *Concluding* exists more in reality and is only partly resolvable. This *partly*, though, is the story, for it keeps life going with a degree of cheerfulness. The conflicting and sustaining forces are the same: the organizing spirit of contemporary institutions and a cagey, crusty individualism.

For the two principals of the school set up by the government to produce workers for the bureaucracy, both the deeper anxieties and the smaller ones come from resistance to the regimented society they are trying to sustain. Their sense of disaster centers on the disappearance of two girls. One is found during the day the novel covers, but avoids having to explain by using the "fair," maternalistic rules of the school system. The other, an anonymous orphan named Mary whom nobody seems to know, never appears, but Miss Edge and Miss Baker keep fearing the news that she has been found dead, and keep hoping that her anonymity will minimize the painful investigation by the bureaucracy. Miss Edge, the dominant co-principal, continues to insist that the rest of the girls must have fun at the annual school dance scheduled for the evening. (And, for the girls, the superbly exciting disappearances do add to the fun.) It takes the reader very few pages to see that Miss Edge is a villain, but most of the novel to see that she is a villain heroine.

The chief resister to this caretaking spirit is cagey, eccentric old Mr. Rock, a retired scientist who once made some anonymous but great discovery and is now busy slopping his pigs, cadging food for himself and the pigs from the school kitchen, and chasing a pet goose around the grounds of the chartered estate. Miss Edge covets the cottage he lives in on the edge of the grounds, partly to become mistress of all she surveys and partly to spare the girls the evil influence of the pigs and the old man, whom they of course like. Mr. Rock, though oppressed by a vision of finding Mary's body in the pond on his way back from chasing the goose, worries chiefly that he will be forced out of his cottage by election to membership in a home for retired scientists. (He resists Miss Edge's efforts to get him elected by stuffing the society's letter into a trunk along with the other unopened letters he has kept for years.)

Green's sterner comedy depends again upon cross-purposes and contradictions in personality. Mr. Rock's daughter, Liz, is recuperating from a mental illness caused by "overwork" in a government bureau, but shows stamina in pursuing Sebastian, a teacher in the school. Sebastian, worried about his masculinity in this feminine environment, wants to marry her and get a better job, but also wants not to marry anybody and stay where he is. Liz is even willing to sacrifice Mr. Rock's cottage to her plans. Both Sebastian and Liz, like Miss Edge and Miss Baker, worry about ratings and the whimsical distant bureaucracy in London. Miss Edge threatens continually to do something drastic about Mr. Rock and the pigs, Miss Baker continually reminds her of channels to be gone through, but Miss Baker panics and upsets the system by bringing in Merode's aunt to complicate the problem of the runaways. Miss Edge wants the girls to like her, but Mr. Rock is initiated into their "secret" club of rebels. Mr. Rock is taken to the dance uninvited, by Liz, but has fun and rejects a proposal of marriage from Miss Edge, who has tried to solve her frustrations about marriage and the cottage in a final bold scheme.

Like *Loving, Concluding* leaves the reader feeling that he missed something. Almost every reader believes he must have skipped the page which tells what happened to the missing girl. But even more primary dramatic considerations are unclear. Why does Green choose a retired old man, scrambling for a living after a distinguished career, as his hero? Why does Miss Edge come through so equivocally—so clearly the villain, yet with an odd heroic proportion? Is the novel a reversion to cynicism about loving?

The three hundred girls, so anonymous that all their names begin with M, carry the theme of love as potential. It is the chief threat to Miss Edge's system of rules—is, in fact, what the rules propose to suppress. These girls at the budding stage are attractive, flirtatious, and hopeful in spite of their circumstances— anonymous copies, almost, of Edith and Kate. Since there are no Raunces around, they seize on whatever they can for excitement. Moira flirts with Mr. Rock while she watches him slop the pigs. (Miss Edge is not wholly wrong in believing that the pigs give her girls wrong ideas.) The runaway Merode contrives to have Sebastian find her, under a tree, with a recently bared leg.

She settles luxuriously into the warm bath that Marchbanks provides on her return. The girls induct Mr. Rock into their secret
society in the basement and want to play kissing games. Even
the principals apparently tolerate the society as a safety valve
for these nonutilitarian emotions.

Against this potential Green sets a devalued image of love between Sebastian Birt and Elizabeth. Sebastian's continual imitations of other people's voices and accents indicate that he does
not know who he is. Elizabeth's love is distrustful, troublesome,
and capricious. Neither lover believes himself lovable, yet for different reasons they will presumably marry and face together the
uncertainties of their futures. Adams, the handyman, furnishes
another devalued symbol, the "dirty old man," Mr. Rock's ma-
lign counterpart. No one knows whether the girls really slip out
to Adams in the woods at night, but their talk shows another side
of loving in their confined situation.

Love as potential, then, is poetic and merry, the hope of the
world; but the only adult love in the novel seems intractable,
neurotic, sometimes silly. Yet the temptation to read Sebastian
and Elizabeth as a prediction for the girls is wrong. Like the missing Mary, the couple represent a threat. Unlike the girls, they
have accepted the organization world. Sebastian's imitations are
his joke against the system, but they are also a joke against him.
He twists his personality to fit the system; he is a different person with Edge, with Winstanley, with Mr. Rock, with Elizabeth.
Elizabeth, too, wants only to fit into a corner of the organization, even if she has to sacrifice her grandfather to do it. So she
and Sebastian do not so much represent adult love as the threat
of trying to make peace without exerting any personal force.
They hope to slide through the organization world without
bringing its power down on them. Neither Mr. Rock nor the
girls have yet accepted this defeatism. Merode's shrewdness in
using the rules to outwit the managers is one of many episodes
promising that no organization can quite confine the spirited.

Mr. Rock, though, seems involved with neither the girls' hope
nor the young adults' compromise. Kingsley Weatherhead has
shown the importance of growth in Green's earlier heroes—Max
in *Party-Going,* Charley Summers in *Back,* Raunce in *Loving.*

But Green deliberately puts Mr. Rock past the stage of any obvious growth. Mr. Rock's object is to maintain life against the approaching threat of death, not to advance. Yet in him Green tests the possibility of loving at a stage when the future no longer promises to be better than the present.

Rock is a hero maimed by age, but akin nevertheless to the many other maimed heroes of modern fiction. His wound acts as a defense against the managing women, and there he is willing to make much of it. Otherwise, he ignores it. He has his affections and, even more, his sense of responsibility. His work is taking care of unmated animals—Daisy, the pig in the pen; Ted, the earthbound goose; the ranging cat; and Elizabeth. He approves of the animals thoroughly, of Elizabeth very little, but he feels responsible for her. Significantly, though, he will not and probably cannot exert authority over her, even to forbidding Sebastian's staying overnight. He can only be grumpy. Yet by the end of the novel Elizabeth seems well on her way to marrying, Daisy is happily asleep in her pen, Ted flies, and the cat comes home.

But Mr. Rock gets some reward. He pleases his animals, and he sees himself clearly as lovable to those capable of loving. The girls want him in their secret society. They believe him on their side in spite of his age, and he is. He does love and cherish; he does not impose authority. He does the dirty work and rejects entirely the public image of eminent, outmoded scientist. He has had a good day "living in the present."

The novel as a whole shows authority extending itself into every detail of conduct, all in the name of responsibility for the future. The drama deals with ways of bearing this burden of being responsible—not, as in *Loving*, with the discovery that responsibility is easier to achieve than to bear. Mr. Rock is the good burden bearer, Miss Edge the bad. She opposes her authority of rules to his authority as a person able to command by example. But the bad has its human side; life is not a melodrama. Miss Baker, the other co-principal, is maternal and cautious, more aware of the prohibitions in the rules than their use for imposing the will. Miss Edge's consciousness will not organize itself around her will. Green makes her human in much the same way that Faulkner makes Mink Snopes human in *The Hamlet*. Miss Edge has tried to impose her will without much thought about consequences, believing only in her own form of right, but, faced with Mary's disappearance, she suffers hallucinatory fears and "sees" Mary's body among the greenery piled up for decorations. Her efforts at control during the lunch, when she feels all the girls watching her, inevitably produce sympathy. Green gives her the apprehensions as well as the irritability attending the life of the will. And though the dance—without men—is an imposed, misguided form of gaiety, Miss Edge carries it through in spite of her own confusion.

But why do we never find what happened to Mary? The answer has already been implied. Mary represents the permanent threat of outbreak against repressive conditions—in the school and in living itself. Finding Merode, who halfheartedly ran away, half solves the problem, which can never be more than half solved. So Mary, like the lost ring in *Loving*, provides a continuing spur for each character's apprehensions. When Miss Edge's frustrated aggressiveness approaches the point of outbreak, the doll in the shrubs seems to her Mary's body. In her calmer moments, she prefers to believe that Mary has run off with a man and hopes to turn this suspicion against Mr. Rock. She fears most of all an "investigation" from London. For Mr. Rock himself, the man with no future, the suicide threat remains the most important face of Mary. He fears finding her in the pond, and yet thinks it ought to be dragged. For Sebastian and Elizabeth, Mary's disappearance means an upset that may start arbitrary authority off on some course dangerous to them. Miss Winstanley, the teacher with few pleasures and hopes, finds in Mary one more prohibition: Miss Edge has forbidden swimming in the pond. There is, in *Concluding*, no way either to find Mary or to get rid of her. She is a protean burden that all the characters must carry.

The depression and threat in the novel are fairly earned. Green's animosity toward organization and aggressive women, as well as his admiration for individuality which manages to maintain itself, is more open here. But, though Miss Edge's determination to keep organized fun going is grimly comic, it also comes through as real. Better grim fun in the face of the disturbing than not carrying on at all—and her decision to go on with the dance in spite of her hallucination is one of Green's memorable scenes.

Mr. Rock does a little better than merely maintain his individuality. In spite of his absurdities, he is an idealized father, debarred from taking his opportunities for love, considered a menace by the managing women, doing the dirty work and expecting only a little admiration and affection. The cook forgets his breakfast, but he eventually gets it—and some slop for Daisy. He resents his granddaughter's conduct, but gets a little affection from Moira. He has a puzzling conflict with Adams and suffers genuine apprehension about Mary, but has a *succès d'estime* as an uninvited guest and refuses Miss Edge's offer of marriage. At the end of the day he still has his cottage, and Miss Edge is doubtless planning some new threat to it. He fears going home in the dark, which means loneliness and death to him, but Elizabeth, who does not fear the dark just now, helps him home. A day of checks and balances.

So *Concluding* concludes nothing. The characters are projected forward into some tomorrow. If the analysis so far is true, it is equally impossible to conclude a chapter on Green. The summary is in the *-ing*.

CHAPTER SIX

Directed Restlessness

JOYCE CARY

JOYCE CARY is Britain's best contemporary popular novelist. Not that he merely sells well—even *Ulysses* sells fairly well—but he writes what readers are prepared to accept. He does not create much pressure toward self-recognition. He is for freedom, imagination, mother, vitality—and who is not? Most first-rate novels confront an intensely felt wish with a resistance that at least recalls the resistance we ourselves meet in the real world. Cary specializes in the intensely felt wish, and in that sense he is popular. Yet he develops this part of experience with a convincingness uncommon in any period.

In his preface to the 1860 edition of *Leaves of Grass*,* Roy Harvey Pearce contends that modern literature needs more joy of Whitman's kind. This demand has appeared elsewhere, notably in recent poetry, but the importance of Pearce's argument derives from his historical awareness. He sees both joy and anguish as forms of self-consciousness, the one dominant in the nineteenth century, the other in the twentieth. Twentieth-century literature has concentrated so much on anguish, however, that it has omitted the possibility of joy. Hence the need for a new vision.

Even saying the word *joy* over a few times, however, suggests the difficulty it has making its way in the present. It calls for a transcendent effort harder than Whitman's. Cary takes his importance largely from making the effort and, in at least one novel, making it effectively. The good feeling that Gulley Jim-

* Introduction to facsimile edition of the 1860 text (Ithaca: 1961) .

son works for in *The Horse's Mouth* is a Whitmanesque joy in creativity. Yet, in contrast to the beat writers, Cary goes about trying to make this joy prevail in the only way that it can possibly prevail now—by subjecting it, as Kenneth Burke would say, to the test of the ridiculous. Gulley retains his hold on the reader by his irony about himself, his imperfect recognition of obstacles, and his canniness in trying to transcend them.

Cary goes further than Green in showing that people like Gulley, who ought not to be enjoying life, are enjoying it, but he does not deal so sharply with the pain in their lives. His characters often meet their difficulties by ignoring them—and so does Cary. Sara, Tabitha, and Gulley all try to transcend problems by submerging them in their own excitement, and this excitement rather than the pain remains in the reader's mind. In fact, much of Cary's appeal lies in this "natural" method of meeting reverses. Characters like Sara, Tabitha, and Gulley do not suffer from severe inner contradictions. They merely direct their inherent restlessness toward fighting circumstances.

Cary's unique comfortableness proceeds from his sense that, though events may be unpredictable, character is not. The restless will rises to meet challenge and begins anew to shape things to its obsession. Sara, Cary's "nest builder," rebuilds her nest every time it is torn down. Gulley responds similarly to discovering that his painting now covers a hole in the roof. Tabitha makes the same point as Sophia in Bennett's *The Old Wives' Tale:* life does not change a strong-willed woman very much. The reader can remain confident through all the characters' troubles because Cary establishes confidence in them. They will meet difficulties in orthodox or unorthodox ways, but they will not stagnate. For all their eccentricities, they stand squarely for the middle-class virtues of drive and applied intelligence. Unlike Hartley, Cary does not defeat his characters in advance; his people do not become senile.

Cary's temperamental affinity, then, is not with Green's mixed world, but with Huxley's and Waugh's all-or-nothing gambles. Cary's comic heroes and heroines, like Waugh's, glorify impulse. They are restless, rebellious, reckless. But Cary gives them two crucial shifts of emphasis. Though they may use fashions for their own purposes, they are individualists who do not stylize their rebellions. And, even more important, Cary wants above all else to reunite impulsiveness with *moral* purpose. Impulse is not its own excuse. The moral purpose may be revolutionizing literature, developing the airplane, mothering homeless men, or reaching a creative ecstasy in painting. The achievement itself may be almost an accident, but Cary wants desperately to show that the restless temperament need not turn to games or self-conscious myths, but by its very existence changes the world. His comic novels could all begin with the same superscription: directed restlessness is the hope of the age.

This directed restlessness is the core of Cary's approach to rapid obsolescence in values. Many of the comic novelists record resistance to change, but, if restlessness is really basic human nature, then people can make common cause with surprise because it is what they too seek. Anthony Powell's hero works to accept his surprises and L. P. Hartley's heroes cannot accept theirs, but many of Cary's main characters celebrate the joys of change. Cary tries to show that there is a fundamental accord between human nature and the shifting styles and ideals of the world at large. To the degree that he succeeds, he evaporates the problem that has vexed his contemporaries.

The novel which shows this effort most explicitly, *A Fearful Joy*, is not a favorite with people who like Cary most. They recognize the heroine, Tabitha Bonser, as one of his best characters, but call the pace too fast. In their view Cary tries to pack in too many revolutions in taste and society, represent too much of twentieth-century history. But rapid revolution is precisely Cary's point. The novel does fade in the last half, not because of its pace, but because of Cary's too determined effort to demonstrate his convictions. In the first half *A Fearful Joy* comes nearer than any other of his novels to making real the accord between human nature and events.

At the beginning Tabitha tires of practicing the piano in a small town and runs off with Bonser, a confidence man who postpones marrying her. She finds him hopelessly irresponsible and flees back home. Home is dull and quarrelsome. She accepts a proposal to become the mistress of a rich businessman turned backer of avant-garde magazines, and in a short time gains control of both backer and magazine. To be avant garde the magazine must be alert to new developments, and new developments turn out to be Tabitha's milieu. She believes in none of the poets and political writers, but she is restless and, with the death of the old Queen, change is in the air. She supports the esthetes to confound her family, then supports the political theorists to confound the esthetes. She compromises on rearing her illegitimate son in order to maintain this atmosphere of exciting and frightening changes. As the title suggests, she is continually anxious—and having the time of her life. When the magazine folds and her backer becomes suddenly too old and harassed to maintain her, she returns home a second time. Since home proves even less welcoming and more quarrelsome than before, she marries an industrialist and spends the next few years amid blueprints, engines, factories, and airplanes. She cares no more for engineering than for literature, but she loves the air of confidence in change that her aging husband provides. The novel carries on rapidly through the next thirty years as Tabitha participates in each new excitement of her son's and granddaughter's lives.

Tabitha fits the rapid action perfectly. In the interesting half of the novel she is the born ally of change and her capriciousness matches the capriciousness of events. Change comes about because many people want it to; though Tabitha may not want particular turns that do occur, she represents a caprice that in each generation makes for revolutions. The first half of the novel contains some of Cary's liveliest writing. For reasons I shall come to shortly, the last half moves toward demonstration.

The First Trilogy, Cary's most important work, consists of two comic novels separated by one in which comedy is incidental. The division follows directly from the main characters' attitudes toward change. Tom Wilcher, the old man who narrates *To Be a Pilgrim,* has spent his life opposing it and seeing it happen. He records with melancholy admiration his brothers' and sisters' attempts to meet life head-on. By contrast, the heroine of *Herself Surprised* and the hero of *The Horse's Mouth* are geniuses of resiliency. In Cary's work only such people make the comic mode and conciliation possible. Tom Wilcher must be treated sadly.

To many novelists, members of the opposite sex seem to meet their problems instinctively, without real struggle. Tension occurs within the writer's own sex. *Herself Surprised* builds on this feeling. Sara Monday's ostensible problem is that the world will not condone her gift for mothering lonely men. Convention cannot approve her marrying one shy man, taking on an affair with his best friend, moving to the friend's pet painter, and, when he deserts her, adopting old Tom Wilcher. Yet the reader is never in danger of siding with convention. Sara's virtues as an idealized mother—comforting, matter-of-fact, tolerant of aberration, able to build a home wherever she finds herself—overwhelm her venial sins. Her sins, in fact, always help other people rather than harm them, and so are merely conventional.

As even this summary shows, Sara has unusual talent for making common cause with change. A good cook, she philosophizes, can always get a situation even without a character. Her real problem, insofar as she has one, is that she needs two husbands—one whom she can make feel good, one who can make her feel good. Keeping up the confidence of a timid, rich husband does not absorb her fully and she adds Hickson, the art collector who makes her feel desirable and important. When this situation becomes stable and familial, she falls in with Gulley Jimson, the painter whose charm is that no one can stabilize him. Sara believes that she wants security and children, but she actually wants excitement. Her quarrels and reconciliations with Gulley make for the happiest five years of her life, but, when Gulley leaves her because she wants to make a provider out of him, she catches on at once with Tom Wilcher, who has been in trouble with the police for exhibitionism. She makes him feel human again and moves from cook to mistress to fiancée. But the old conflict recurs. Gulley reappears to cadge, and she steals from Wilcher to give money to Gulley. She ends in jail writing her memoirs for the newspapers, still supporting herself.

As in many of his novels, Cary divides the character of the husband: the cheerful man is unreliable in affections and reckless about money, the good provider is timid and depressed.

Sara tries to solve the dilemma by having two men at the same time, and the difficulties in this juggling provide her only real tension. *Herself Surprised* is a happy book, and women like to recognize themselves in the portrait.

Since *To Be a Pilgrim* is not primarily comic, it does not come into this discussion directly. But the third novel in the trilogy, *The Horse's Mouth,* is Cary's best, and in it Cary faces some of the real obstacles to being in league with the future. Gulley has extraordinary talent for invective against the world, but he also has an inner problem with possibilities. The novel, which seems to run on amiably, actually has an all but mechanical framework. At the beginning, Gulley is an old man angry to the point of depression at the way things have gone, foreseeing a doubtful future. He is "stuck." Unlike some of Green's heroes, he suffers because his obsession is not stronger than it is. Not only is he unable to shut out distractions, but, like a Lypiatt of *Antic Hay* turned merry instead of melancholy, he cannot paint the inspiration he believes himself to have. (His pictures are, significantly, all larger than life size and distorted in a way that the public will not accept.)

In this first stage—symbolized by his effort to paint a huge mural of "The Fall"—he is highly distractable, primarily because he wants revenge upon society for not taking him on his own terms. Also, he is coming to the end of an era. His life has been a history of dependence upon admiring women for support and inspiration. Here, he is depending on Coker, the hard-boiled barmaid "built like a fireplug." Like Sara, she believes in his genius and wants him to achieve; but, unlike Nina, Sara, Rozzie, Lizzie, and the rest, she will not simply nourish her pet. She has problems of her own—an illegitimate child on the way— and wants to be repaid for the money she has lent Gulley. She plans to recapture from Sara the saleable portraits of Sara in her bath. The public will pay for these nudes that Gulley no longer takes an interest in; it will pay nothing for his giant mythological murals. He knows that he cannot go back again and that Sara will withhold the pictures because they mean the real intensity of life to her, but he must put up with the distraction of trying Coker's plan, which of course fails. (Actually, Gulley does not need the nudes; only a nostalgic dependence on Sara makes him believe that he does. When he finally breaks through this illusion, he copies the portrait in the Tate gallery and gets money at once for his less popular art.)

But the wish for pointless revenge is his great distraction. He can appease Coker, steal paints, swindle for canvas, and still go on painting. But he prefers to make nuisance calls to Hickson, who he believes has cheated him, or steal art objects from Hickson's house and hurl them through the windows when he is chased. He sets out to burn down the house when Coker's mother destroys his work. But Cary indulges him in all this cheerfully. In the logic of the novel Gulley has to express this anger, try to control it, and work through it before he can find a genuine inspiration. His opportunity to express the anger comes when he revenges himself against Lady Beeder's riches and amateur spirit by painting huge feet on her apartment wall and allowing a sculptor to finish the destruction. In this second stage, "the land of Beulah," he lives in comfort by pawning everything portable in the apartment, down to the bathroom chain. The Beeders remain infinitely tolerant of such idiosyncrasies of genius, but they want nudes or portraits and the help they offer means nothing to Gulley. Nevertheless, the experience has carried him to a point where he realizes the impossibility of further dependence.

The third stage, when he actually paints "The Creation," shows his break with weakness and his final reliance upon his own obsession. To make the break, he must kill Sara, the ultimate symbol of his dependence. He returns for one more effort to recapture the lost drawings and more or less accidentally pushes her down the stairs while she is defending the remnants of her best days. The crucial scene of the last section shows her reappearing in an hallucination as he paints high on his scaffold. She appeals to the past and his need for her, but he answers, "not now."

'I'm all right, Sall. You've only got to look at me, full of jump.' 'Oh dear, aren't I looking and grieving? Don't I know that you know that you're done for? Come, dearie, give it up. Listen to your

Sara. Didn't I give you comfort and peace often and often when you were fit to be tied with worrying about your greens and your blues and the rest of your nonsense? Yes, even though you did hit me on the nose, weren't you glad to come into my arms after, yes, with the very blood on your pyjamas, and think you were back with your mother again?" "There you go, Sall, you old bluemange, you've thrown away your stays at last and taken the whole world to your bosom.' 'Well, I go on asking myself why can't people be happy, poor dears? Why do they have to go moiling and toiling and worrying each other? Life's too short.' 'Now, Sara, old girl, if you don't mind—' 'And you don't really want me?' 'Not just now, my dear.' 'And aren't you sorry I'm dead?' 'Well, look at me, my dear, boo-hoo, with the tears running down my nose, real tears.' A genuine grief. Yes, I'm sorry you're dead, my dear, and that I'm done for. But after all, we mustn't get too upset, must we? It's the way things are.' 'Oh dear, oh dear, I ought to know what life is.' 'Yes,' I said, putting another touch on the old un's nose, to give it more elevation. 'Practically A MATTER OF LIFE AND DEATH, you might say, or thereabouts.'

He can now move forward frenetically, undistracted, with his creation. The forces of the future, a group of young art students, help. When the philistine government tears down the condemned church wall he has chosen to paint on, his triumph is complete. The survival of the painting means nothing. The ability to imagine and create is all, and Gulley has downed his pointless angers and his clinging to the past. He has achieved his dedication.

The Horse's Mouth, then, presents the hero's strong fantasy of himself and the obstacles to making it prevail in a world with purposes of its own. The apparently rambling story does progress—from self-defeating anger through some release in mockery to artistic celebration, "practically a matter of life and death." Yet imaginative detail so submerges this framework that few admirers of Cary will find it enough to account for the impact of the novel. There is something else.

One something-else is giving the reader all the joys of a scattergun rebellion against family, church, and state without making him leave home. Cary mutes the isolation and loneliness of anarchic individualism, and plays up its fun and warmth.

Whatever the relation of this effect to reality, it appeals power-
fully—especially to young people. (One principle of popular
works like *Brave New World* and *The Horse's Mouth* is undoubtedly giving the reader the best of both worlds.) But the
friendliness and merriment surrounding Gulley make his revolt
very different from what it might otherwise be. He gripes about
the ordinary dissatisfactions—business, the government, mass
taste, critics, and so on—but with a talent for the metaphor-of-
disrespect far beyond most people's. His favorites come from fish
and wild life:

> The people kept floating in. Like fish in an aquarium full of
> dirty brown water, three dimensions of fish faces, every one on top
> of the other. Bobbing slowly to and fro, and up and down. Goggle
> eyes, cod mouths. Hanging in the middle of the brown. Waiting for
> a worm or just suspended. Old octopus in corner with a green dome
> and a blue beak, working his arms, Trying to take off his overcoat
> without losing his chair. Old female in black with a red nose creep-
> ing about in the dark corners like a crawfish, shaking her bonnet
> feathers and prodding her old brown umbrella at the chairs.
> Young skate stuck up the wall with bulgy white eyelids and a little
> white mouth. Never moving. You'd think he was glued to the side
> of the tank.

The skate turns out to be Plantie's prize American professor, the
speaker of the evening. Professor Alabaster appears thus:

> He wasn't a detective. Though he wore a neat brown suit and a
> brown hat. He had too long a neck and he turned out his toes. He
> was walking like the front legs of a French pug. He had round
> shell spectacles and his expression was intellectual as well as watch-
> ful. That is to say, he looked so that any good vet. would have
> said, at a first glance, that poor dog has worms.
> What does that poor animal want with me, I wondered. Can he
> be a brother artist? He looks as if he might be capable of a wash-
> drawing in sepia; or decorating book-ends with transfers.
> Suddenly the young man gave his neck a twist, as if to shake a
> fly out of his ear; his large brown eyes, melting like jelly on a
> warm afternoon, filled with respectful delight, and off came his
> chappo. 'Excuse me, sir, but are you, by any chance, Mr. Gulley
> Jimson? I called at your studio twice last week.'

Any claim of authority guarantees its professor a place in Gulley's aquarium or zoo.

The warmth evolves with great inventiveness. In many recent comic novels—Green's, Powell's, Hartley's—the hero becomes comic through his actions and stance, but does not think of himself as a comedian. Gulley does. He is also, of course, one of the few painters in literature who show a sustained visual imagination, and the novel is full of passages like

> The moon was coming up somewhere, round the corner from the side bow window, making the trees like fossils in a coalfield, and the houses look like fresh-cut blocks of coal, glittering green and blue; and the river banks like two great solid veins of coal left bare, and the river sliding along like heavy oil. It was like a working model of the earth before somebody thought of dirt, and colours and birds and humans. I liked it even better than the dome of glory. I liked it so much that I wanted to go out and walk about in it. But of course I knew it wouldn't be there. You never get the real world as solid as that. It was a trick of the light. Alfred's old white cat, jumping on the wall, spoilt the weight of it. I had to put up my can to blot her out.

But to this central claim for the self Gulley adds the less overt, but even more sustained, claim of the comedian, the half-detached discoverer of his own distress and absurdity. He constantly plays for laughs—and profits from a cast of idealists who act as straight men for his deflationary realism. Monologue of the same sort gives him a second art, to which he is as dedicated as he is to painting. Open almost any page of the novel, and this alertness to contradiction between the ideal and the horse's mouth real appears:

> There was a street market on the kerb. Swarms of old women in black cloaks jostling along like bugs in a crack. Stalls covered with blue-silver shining pots, ice-white jugs, heaps of fish, white-silver, white-green, and kipper gold; forests of cabbage; green as the Atlantic, and rucked all over in permanent waves. Works of passion and imagination. Somebody's dream girls. Somebody's dream pots, jugs, fish. Somebody's love supper. Somebody's old girl chasing up a titbit for the old china. The world of imagination is the world of eternity. Old Sara looking at a door knob. Looking at my old ruins. The spiritual life.

His comedian's skill transforms the potentially painful into the joke already recognized and accepted years ago—make pain homey, lived with, worn out. (His age, 67, adds plausibility.) This page-by-page transformation, even more than the main movement, validates Gulley's declaring, "I'm an optimist. I get a lot of fun out of fun, as well as the miseries." He gets a lot of fun out of broad clowning, too.

Point of view is crucial to the effect. At first glance the interior monologue resembles Leopold Bloom's in *Ulysses*, though Gulley obviously has a greater sense of direction. But his monologue, instead of being direct and immediate, recreates past events as Gulley lies in a hospital bed dictating to his "honorary secretary." He thus appears to think, joke, and readjust much more rapidly than Bloom—does not grope toward comic perceptions, but gives them a sharp, formed, literary turn:

> Then the door opened and I saw the copper and the man coming out; and old Hickson waving his fins like a penguin in despair. So I sent the last box, a heavy diamond one, at his head, and ran for it.
>
> I'm sixty-seven, but I'm light and I can still run. I might have beaten that copper if he hadn't blown his whistle. But then coppers started up all round me. They seemed to come out of the street gratings, and drop from the sky. And they all took hold of me at once and nearly pulled my arms off.
>
> 'That's enough,' I said. 'Be careful what you're doing. I'm Mister Gulley Jimson, and I shall put this matter into my lawyer's hands. First-class lawyers. For false imprisonment and assault. Obviously you don't know who I am. Call a taxi.'
>
> I got six months for this piece of carelessness. I knew I was making a mistake when I put those snuff-boxes in my pocket, just to get them off the table. And foolishness when I lost my temper. Blood pressure is one of my worst enemies. A traitor in the camp. It would be too good a joke to let him blow my brains out from the inside.

This rapidity provides the characteristic sense of movement even when nothing much is happening. The second law of motion in *The Horse's Mouth* comes from making a principle of surprise. For its sake Gulley recklessly deals out apparent con-traditions. Though his individualism has a core—a liquid one, perhaps—he never risks the vice of small minds. He loves all the paradoxes: denounce the rich, and defend Hickson, the Beeders, and the whole "sausage machine" as necessary for art. Though his claims for recognition are gigantic, he loves to surprise his serious supporter Plantie.

But, of course, Plantie wouldn't listen to me. He has a lot of old English feelings under all his foreign philosophies, just as he has a lot of the real old English religion under all his fandangos. He loves to fight the law. 'No, no,' he said, 'no compromise with those rascals.' And he got up meetings and took subscriptions till my name stank for miles round. And he hired that lawyer G----, who looked like a crystallized choirboy, only his head was quite bald. He came to see me in my old studio and when I had told him all about myself and my little jokes, he said, 'I see, Mr. Jimson, we'll have to concentrate on character.' 'No, you haven't,' I said. 'Remember I'm an artist. And you know what that means in a court of law. Next worst to an actress.' 'That's what I mean,' he said. 'And I believe you're a modern artist.' 'Very nearly,' I said. 'Yes,' he said, 'it's a difficult case. We can only stick to character and hope for the best.' And when he got into court he began at once to throw dirt on Hickson. It was wonderful. That man was a poet. The way he made it seem that poor old Hickie had been a bloodsucker in buying my pictures cheap, and that he'd been exploiting poor devils like me all his life.

He plays the same trick over and over on Nosy.

But there is also a direct atmosphere of friendliness. Sara's affection over the years and Gulley's intermittent return of it go along with other kinds of warmth. Gulley emanates it, and is surrounded by it; for an angry old man, he has amazingly successful personal relations. His enemies are authority figures on the edges of the narrative; all the characters with any definition love him. (When one bar acquaintance threatens not to, Gulley retreats to saying that ideas differ and there is nothing to quarrel about.) The bond of common beat-up humanity is more real than opinion. He explains his friends' occasional prickliness biographically—Coker is homely, Plantie has been shot up in the war. Again Gulley achieves the best of both worlds: he has all the individualist's freedom to complain while being surrounded by a coterie of well-wishers who do not try to enforce conformity.

Yet Cary does not depend on mere wish fulfillment; he shows a way in which the paradox could work. In fact, his finest perceptions—as distinguished from his entertainment—show how a mind so involved in a fantasy of self operates. In the sense that many novelists create a world, there is none in *The Horse's Mouth*. Gulley's self-absorption, his inability to take a sustained interest in others, makes for a fitful and shadowy outer reality. Critics often speak of Cary's talent for character; yet in this novel the test of a character's existence is his ability to capture Gulley's attention, and the only claim on Gulley's attention is some resemblance to himself and his situation.

Thus the young sculptor and his wife who join Gulley in the apartment catch his interest. The girl models for hours—naked, teeth chattering—without having the smallest faith in her husband's talent. She is keeping him happy. Gulley and the sculptor return from the tavern to find her still stiffened in her pose, and have to call a doctor to uncrook her. Gulley sees in her an ideally compliant Sara (Sara herself was apt to be capricious about "showing a leg"). The sculptor attracts Gulley because he has gone on binges, jumped off bridges, and hanged himself at times when he has been "stuck." Gulley only goes on binges, but he understands.

Plantie, the shoe repairman who preaches a social gospel to a little group of eccentrics, is another reflector. Gulley also likes to preach to fellow eccentrics about the wrongs of the world; but Plantie is just different enough to hold Gulley's interest as a lesson as well as a person. Gulley sees in his losing a hand through infection and becoming a pauper the moral to accept no comfort whatever about the way the world goes. Plantie, who is kindly and wants to believe the best, suffers the most. (Yet he, like Gulley, makes a place for himself in a world that has no place for him. He becomes a dignitary by controlling the key to the men's room in the flophouse where he lives.)

Nosy, the young hanger-on, becomes a character by the difficulty he has in gaining Gulley's attention. But when he has proved himself by ignoring discouragement, he becomes for

Gulley the artist in embryo, as Andrew Wright calls him—unable to listen to reason about family, career, or girls. Gulley sees him as his own successor in abandoning the happy office job for the curse of painting.

When Gulley does not see the resemblance he is looking for, there are no characters. Significantly, though he is at his funniest in complaining about the hostile world, the characters who represent it are the shadowiest of all. Incident is everything. The police, the town councillors, and the young tough who throws Gulley off his dirty postcard route have the flatness of characters in jokes. Sir William and his lady are prop representatives of "the rich" for Gulley to bounce witticisms off. Their apartment is far more real than they are. Even Hickson, the art collector, is a simple type surrounded with a little warmth from long association.

Gulley sees objects in even more direct relation to his fantasy of himself. His painting on walls and his stealing are both ways of dealing with barriers, which he now sees everywhere. In his Sara-in-her-bath period, he did not notice walls at all. He acted on a faith that no one could stop him—neither Sara nor Hickson nor the government nor bill collectors. Now they have all stopped him. Since he is "stuck" in painting on canvas, he quits stealing it and uses the walls which exist all around him. He tries, in other words, to transform a barrier into a thing of beauty and a joy forever. He puts his faith in creativity to transcend the solidest limits, and so cannot stand a bare wall. The Beeders are only interesting specimens to him, but their apartment wall is the novel's best symbol for Gulley's combination of destructive and creative.

Painting the huge mural of "The Creation" in the condemned church brings on a kind of walls-of-Jericho exhilaration. Gulley says at one point, in mock exasperation, that he has only to start painting on a wall to make it come tumbling down. His highest excitement occurs when his whale seems to smile at him as the plaster cracks. Destructive and creative are inseparable for Gulley, and part of his triumph comes from the magnificent crash. His painting has apparently had the power to mobilize the whole force of organized society—specifically, the town councillors—against him and thus make him an enemy worthy of its attention. Even the Beeders attend the crash.

The stealing is his utilitarian mode of overcoming barriers. Though Gulley has several confidence tricks—distracting the shopkeeper to get paints, using others' imagination to sell "filthy pictures" of unexceptionable churches—he breaks through practical limits chiefly by taking what he "deserves." He steals the paints from a shopkeeper as poor as he is. Since Hickson has denied him further money, he takes the art objects. He collects his advance on the Beeders' uncommissioned mural by pawning their furniture. He commandeers the abandoned church in the face of warnings about its imminent destruction. Stealing—taking—is the criminal form of transcending limits that in its benign form inspires his art. And, significantly, he counts on his victims' being as self-absorbed as he is and thus distracted from what is going on before them.

The churches symbolize another part of his feeling about himself. The filthy picture buyers want nudes, just as the art collectors do. Gulley wants to give them religious pictures. He chooses in the condemned church another representative of his own predicament. He is preaching a disregarded religion—Blake and art, in his case—to a congregation of town councillors and *voyeurs*.

Such interweavings give *The Horse's Mouth* a special quality. The structure, like the structure of the trilogy itself, is almost static; the sensitive detail all but conceals the shell. There is nothing inevitable about Gulley's progress from the fall to the creation—it is more like a miracle. But there is a heterodox logic to the ins and outs of Gulley's mind.

In general, Cary has had a good press. The disposition to believe what he believes is strong. Critics have attributed to him many virtues and a few weaknesses, largely forgivable. (Narrowness is the most common.) He has so much good-heartedness and merry dissatisfaction that it is hard to subject him to questions; yet in the absence of firmer judgment he is likely to lapse from our attention as a good man not quite relevant to present conflicts. For Cary has one weakness that is hard to forgive completely. He is often dull.

The dullness is not an accident; its causes lie at the heart of his work. *The Horse's Mouth* is harder to reread than most comic novels. The excitement and perceptions are there; they are not illusions. But Cary often mixes in Gulley's ramblings without bringing these into any meaningful relation to the novel as a whole. The lively periods are intermittent, and between them Cary doodles. Yet when he tries, as in the last half of *A Fearful Joy*, to speed up the pace, he loses his spontaneous perception and becomes too demonstrative. He can never wholly integrate his simplified framework with sustained play of mind. (Cary's statement that he wrote the big scenes first and then filled in between seems external confirmation of the difficulty.)

The problem is not one of mere lapses. Cary continues the line of Huxley and Waugh—life as programmatic excitement. Where they probe the internal limits of the ideal, Cary tries desperately to find it without real limits. What Cary does is to transform the program of excitement from frivolous and casually destructive styles to moral purpose and religious yearning. (Even in *To Be a Pilgrim*, where Tom Wilcher is passive, the novel takes its interest from his resisting others' energy or falling in behind it.) Significantly for this program of excitement, Cary found himself as a novelist during and immediately after the war. His dull passages are an involuntary recognition of the limits inherent in his program, and as such they lie inert in his novels, beyond the author's control.

In other words, Cary becomes dull frequently because he can find no comic interest in the life of necessity. Conditions that must be lived with or fought against unsuccessfully do not engage his comic imagination, and he only recognizes that they exist. (In the trilogy as a whole, *To Be a Pilgrim* provides this perspective, but the comic novels themselves do not.) Andrew Wright has called Cary an existentialist writer, but this is true of the novels discussed here only in the narrowest sense. Cary endorses the optimism about commitment, it is true, but he engages far too lightly the Nothingness from which Being takes its meaning. He tries to show, in direct contradiction to Sartre, that Nothingness is ultimately unreal.

Cary continues the tradition of first-generation twentieth-century novelists whose preference for extremes, as Lionel Trilling has said, tries to make life into pure spirit. For the time being, at least, he is the last comic novelist of his kind in England. Spirit colliding with the given is now having its day. Logically, Cary should have followed Huxley and Waugh in this book, but the chapter on Green shows that, while Cary was achieving popularity by expanding a traditional conflict, another novelist had already shifted the scene. Yet saying that Cary transforms an established action, or that he sometimes writes dully, does not diminish him seriously; it may make possible a more accurate understanding of his achievement.

CHAPTER SEVEN

The
Unconfident Confidence Man

TOWARD THE PRESENT

THE IMPOSTOR WAS a stock character in comedy when Terence left Africa, and as the rogue has been in the comic novel from the first. Nothing about him can be purely modern. Yet for this very reason his contemporary form becomes an economical device for measuring our sense of ourselves and our age against a visible past. The recent novelists have extended the range of this stockest of stock characters so consistently that a look at their confidence man gives one clue to literary history. (The reader will perhaps bear with going over again some of the evidence in this perspective.)

Though the rogue made his appearance first in the picaresque novel, by the nineteenth century he had already established himself in the novel of manners. Contemporary novelists, highly aware of restrictions upon the individual, have most often put him in scenes where escape to the next episode cannot readily occur. As a result their confidence man, unlike the rogue, has become both anxious and amateur—amateur not only in the sense of for-love-of-the-sport but in the sense of not-very-good-at-it. The cycle of aggression and fear, fear and aggression—which for important reasons had to be excluded from his picaresque form—has become crucial to his character. And a discrepancy between the private self and the public role, always a possibility in the character, has become a conflict no longer masked by the convention of emotional invulnerability.

Robert B. Heilman's excellent analysis of the picaresque novel explains why the earlier novelists excluded real emotions.[*] Heilman sees the rogue as a comic Faust, representing the part of the personality devoted to controlling the environment. The rogue is therefore the supreme rationalist, who lives by wit, charm, and scheme, and denies all emotions that inhibit his aggressive impulses. His half-crimes proceed effortlessly—and more or less harmlessly—in order to purge the reader's guilt about his own aggressiveness. The conventional prison term before retirement on the nest egg satisfies the reader's suspicion that even cheerful crime ought not to pay too well.

One change recent novelists have made in the confidence man seems simple after the fact. Like the serious novelists, they have taken the inner life as real. They worry about aggressiveness that the rogue once purged in the reader has now become the character's own chief problem. A natural as well as a social barrier to the ideal of control has arisen, and the conventional punishment has become both internal and automatic. Further, to add to his confusion and contribute to his amateurishness, the modern confidence man has had to question far more than his predecessors the purposes of control itself. A suspicion that his goals are worthless so haunts him that he constantly tests his ratio of pleasure to pain.

The briefest check will show how recent the change has been. Heilman analyzes *The Confessions of Felix Krull* as a great modern picaresque novel showing both the character and the effect. Mann, however, could continue the rogue tradition because, as he has said, he grew up in the nineteenth century and his works celebrate the bourgeois spirit. In Forster's pre-World-War-I novels, with their ideal of honest and imaginative self-management, the confidence man barely appears; the ideal excludes him. Bennett's *The Card*, another celebration of the bourgeois spirit, shows the usual merry hero. But *Antic Hay*, published shortly after the war, brings the trickster into some collision with his own fears and hints at a conflict of public and private selves. Gumbril has vague apprehensions, and genuine

* "Variations on Picaresque (*Felix Krull*)," *Sewanee Review*, LXVI (Autumn, 1958).

grounds for self-doubt. His false beard transforms him from the "weak, silent man" Mrs. Viveash knows to the Complete Man who charms Rosie and successfully promotes Gumbril's Patented Small Clothes. But he can use the beard only to impose on the casually gullible; he cannot trust it when his feelings become involved with the skittish Emily. The Complete Man, like the Monster in the night club act, is actually a mode of self-mockery.

Huxley's disguise convention spells out a conflict that develops more subtly in later comic novels. The beard creates an ideal self that the confidence man cannot believe in except as others believe in it. There remains his private, devalued image of the self—the "weak, silent man"—yearning for the tenderness that Emily promises. Gumbril alternates between the two images of himself, marking them off clearly from each other. Huxley thus emphasizes the fear of weakness from which the confidence role arises. His hero can meet the problem only by coming to terms with Mrs. Viveash.

Complete, though, is a key word. Gumbril's hopes for his beard resemble childhood fantasies of omnipotence. With it he hopes to seduce beautiful girls, get rich through his invention, and live in lazy happiness. This combination of strong fantasies with unwillingness to work toward long-term fruition is basic in the impostor. Gumbril does not want to teach history or study architecture or romanticize women; he wants instant success—and domination. He remains human because he treats the Complete Man as partly a joke. Laughing at it and keeping it as a sideline preserve him from great anxiety.

Waugh's heroes, though, believe more seriously in their fantasies of power. When these collide with the real world, the hero admits being stopped, and turns to outrageous revenges upon a society that will not accept his wish for omnipotence. This turning creates a much stronger anxiety than Gumbril's (Cary also shows this revenge for a destroyed fantasy.) In Waugh, Huxley's hints become an open conflict of public and private selves. Critics usually refer to Paul Pennyfeather and Adam Sykes as innocents in a corrupt world, but they are so only if innocence means inexperience and sensitivity rather than intent. They mean to be competent confidence men. Paul begins well enough, but falls in with the hope of using his charm for Lady Metroland to make his way in the chromium world. Until late in the novel he does not have enough perception to notice his anxiety, but he is amateur all through. When he finds it impossible to combine scheming with sensitivity, he retires via prison to the university.

Adam, as has been said, is a portrait of uncertainty trying to appear vital and assured. Like the other members of his coterie, he wants to establish a spectacular public personality to down his private confusion, and the action of the novel shows a race between anxiety and a contrived gaiety. The anxiety centers around a fear of the exhibitionism that gives the group its sense of being alive—is, indeed, only the obverse of its idea. Adam begins his confidence game as a way of getting along without income, but, in becoming a gossip columnist, the official historian of the exhibitionists, creates illusion on a large scale. He is a confidence man for kicks—taking other people in is great fun —but the game produces its own fears. Since it depends on inventiveness and public approval, he becomes afraid of losing both, and does lose his job over the unsuccessful fad for green bowler hats. Even more serious, because he is trying to deceive so many people, he fears most being taken in himself. In his society the confidence man has much to worry about from other confidence men.

Basil Seal, in *Black Mischief,* bases his success as a confidence man on disgust with the tame, stylized society around him. His actions are fantastic, but his disgust is real, and his campaign to modernize Azania under a slogan of Sterility foreshadows Tony Last's desertion of the society in *A Handful of Dust.*

In Huxley and Waugh, then, the confidence man shows a tension between pretended and real, between a way of acting which promises *faute de mieux* satisfactions and a muted demand for integrity. The tension, peculiarly suited to its period, arises partly because the characters are *inventing* new patterns of conduct. They feel all the uncertainties of the untried. They rebel against Edwardian mores because they consider the past absurd, and respond by trading absurdity for absurdity. But in Waugh especially the fear develops that this weapon may not be serious enough to command attention.

Many others held this view of it, and of these Henry Green gave the confidence man his most important turn. His *Party-Going* (1939), written late in the cycle of party-going novels, treats the bright young people as children who must either grow up or wither in dependence. In destroying older ways and establishing their own styles, they have achieved only claustrophobic boredom. No one in *Party-Going* has enough energy to be a confidence man. (Whatever his defects, he is a moving spirit in his society.) Green accepts cheerfully enough that old ways are changing, control is passing from the apathetic to the vital, but he does not, like Waugh, view this with any special horror. For him the past, good or bad, is there and cannot be exorcised by childish rebellion any more than it can be maintained intact because Edwardian ladies like it. The only adult course is to integrate present rebelliousness and past practice.

The past survives in *Loving* because the new generation needs it. No character has much personal history, but each takes his identity from an existing pattern of work. After three hundred years, operating a castle in Ireland is a departmentalized routine; the servants can continue even though the owners have lost heart. Huxley and Waugh defend their heroes, a little uneasily, by showing that the competitive world creates the role of confidence man and individuals merely step into it. Green accepts this idea as a fact needing no defense. Raunce inherits not only the conception of the confidence game, but detailed instructions for operating it—old Eldon's two little books. Charging for new whiskey bottles while re-using old ones and the like have gone on for so long that they represent the real morality; but they conflict with the official morality, and Raunce's slyness symbolizes the conflict. He cannot carry off the standard procedures with the dignity that old Eldon gave them, and so seems less competent. In the eyes of his employer, his actions are less suspect than his lack of manner. He does not make the impression a confidence man ought to make and so, in Heilman's terms, does not render value received for his cheatings. Nevertheless, he bluffs his way well enough until nominal responsibility evolves into real responsibility.

In Raunce, Green invents the managerial confidence man.

Huxley's and Waugh's heroes are nonconformists who defy ordinary realities and continue the old idea of large-scale deception
—the Complete Man of a nonexistent social whirl. Raunce defies no reality; he wants only to slip around it. He is a manager
rather than a promoter, and the pettiness of his deceptions
emphasizes their tie with the indirections of daily life. In him
the confidence man as miscellaneous rebel changes to the confidence man as manager of a stumbling organization.

Green's image destroyed the Huxley-Waugh one, and pre-
vailed with the younger novelists—diluted, however, by the
curious sentiment of Cary's *The Horse's Mouth*. On the face of
things, Gulley Jimson lives by his wits in order to create his
Blakean vision in art. He tricks for a higher cause—a kind of
religious confidence game. In his view every act from stealing
paints and cadging from the barmaid to ruining the borrowed
apartment contributes to the advancement of British art. (In all
of his games, though, he is amateur enough to doubt, rightly, his
ability to carry them out.)

Cary encourages the reader to take this benign view, but there
is a discrepancy between the Blake quotations and the big scenes
that keep the novel moving. Telephoning Hickson, going with
Coker to rescue the picture, and expropriating the apartment all
portray revenge against an adult world that refuses to understand the child-artist's demand to be supported and recognized
for acting as he pleases. The telephoning does not help Gulley
get along—it has just cost him six months in jail. Instead it
expresses his resentment at a patron who treats him well, but
lacks understanding. When Coker tries to get money for him, he
openly sides with Sara's trickery. He likes seeing the righteous,
bill-paying Coker beaten. The essential confidence man in *The
Horse's Mouth* is not the artist forced to low means of subsist-
ence, but the Bohemian revenging himself upon the patronizing,
upright citizen. Gulley is in part a poetry-quoting Basil Seal,
spiritualizing his destructive impulses.

But only in part, for Gulley recognizes this anger as the enemy
within and tries to talk himself into managing it. He knows it is
the barrier to his ever completing a picture. Also, whereas Gumbril, Adam, and Raunce are all doing what the world tells them

to do. Gulley is a confidence man—and artist—on his own
authority. The world pointedly tells him not to be either. He
does not want to join a coterie or work with others; he is expressing himself. The structure shows him moving from the
futile effort at dependence to living solely on his own, and
when he finally believes that he can live alone he can also complete his painting of the Creation.

What does he stand for, though, when he stands alone? The
good feeling. Man at the top of his bent is a bundle of creative
feelings. The work is incidental. None of the other recent confidence men so divorces sentiment from result.

The younger novelists may admire Cary more, but they accept
Green's world. Their heroes relish a social framework descend-
ing from the past and define themselves within it. And the
tendency in Green for anxiety to be stronger than drive goes even
further in Kingsley Amis. Amis, though, comes closer than anyone else to creating what Cary purports to create—the purely
defensive confidence man. Lucky Jim's idea of management is
refraining. He hates teaching, distrusts intellectual women, fears
bright students, considers medieval history meaningless and
wants only to persuade his music-happy superiors that he loves
all these. The threat of nausea becomes the dominating image in
the novel. The action progresses through not-quite-unscathed
escapes from being unmasked to the point where, if the mask
does not fall, Lucky Jim does. His idea of activity is to avoid
entanglement in Margaret's emotional problems, conceal the
cigarette hole in the bedsheet, evade his professor's interest in
his progress, and get out of directing theses. His relation with
Margaret points up his effort to deal with the managing world
without giving it any loyalty. Apparently the crisis in Margaret's
neurosis comes directly from her effort to fit in while clinging to
her rebelliousness. She dislikes much of what she lives with, but
cannot play the confidence game, and tries to believe. Jim tries
only to down the Bohemian Bertrand and marry an ordinary
girl—further symbols of his protective coloration.

John Braine's Joe Lampton, in *Room at the Top*, uses his
charm and wits more directly, but accepts still more his role of
manager within a solid social framework. He combines the

nineteenth-century figure of the outsider on the make—the orphan—with the con man following a prescription for success—marry the boss's daughter. In the process he develops the anxieties of social mobility. But the best parts of the novel show him making the easy adaptations to the society he wants so much to join. He fits in quickly with better clothes, better bathrooms, better manners, amateur acting, and nude pictures in the living room. But he and his friend Charles have classified men by their income and women by their attractiveness on a one-to-ten scale, and his civil service position means at best number six-mediocrity. (Number six men have number six to number nine wives.) Joe does not question the rightness of this scale; he merely determines to become a number two man with a number one wife. For him the touching Susan means simply status; part of his embarrassment comes from her taking him as a real person.

The action of the novel shows this status conflict mixing with his attraction to both maternal and daughterly women. He makes his easiest and most natural alliance, as a newcomer in the society, with a nonconformist older woman. He shifts from her to Susan, back to her, back again to Susan in a conflict between his rationalist ambitions and his feelings. But, though he wants to do the extraordinary thing, he again does not question the reasonableness of the rules that demand the correct choice rather than the comfortable one. He only regrets the impossibility of having the best of both. After choosing Susan and becoming a number two man, he feels himself a "clothes-horse," a masquerader who has denied the affections and tried to integrate himself by intellect alone.

As a group, contemporary comic novelists achieve a partial *modus vivendi* with the confidence man. They have played up the anxieties, angers, and doubts about worth that attend the rational effort to control the environment. They have exploited the cycle of aggression and fear, fear and aggression, and, most important, have pictured the distortion of personality involved in the attempt to team the public and the private selves. In the cultural context, they provide symbols for changing values. The confidence man has shifted from a 1920's rebel doing to society no more than it deserves for being as absurd as it is to a manager who does what is expected of him and regrets the price. The two progressions have all but removed the criminal aspect of the character. Aggressive acts that conscience once suspected as crime become human nature and the way of the world. The world hurries the protagonist toward the role rather than deterring him, and his punishment comes from inner conflict and the limits of the ideal itself. The scenes of action are well away from petty crime—parties, the world of work. Instead of asking the reader to recognize himself in the illegitimate, the novelists have moved the confidence man nearer the norm and asked the reader to laugh directly at his own aggressiveness and fantasies of omnipotence.

The rogue, in other words, has become partly at home in the more fixed world of the novel of manners. He has lived there for a long time, but deceivers like Wickham and Frank Churchill in the party-going world of Jane Austen and Mr. Slope in the organization world of Trollope oppose the values of the novels; in the contemporary novel of manners the deceiver also embodies the values. Roguery and honesty, aggression and conscience exist side by side in the hero, who could almost be defined as a man able, but barely able, to live within the code of some group.

Though retaining much of his old purgative function for the reader, the confidence man has become a subtler and more socially acceptable fellow. Much of modern literature and thought has engaged in reducing conscience from an idea of perfection to something nearer human possibility. The confidence man plays his part in this reduction by creating an awareness of the inevitable pull between "rational" planning and its emotional resisters. He does directly for the reader what the rogue of earlier fiction did indirectly. For all his outrageous acts, he has become less embarrassing to the public while becoming more human, less instrumental, more embarrassed himself. Apparently the world lives less surreptitiously with its ambiguous wish to master the environment.

The novelists of the fifties make this normalization explicit. Since Huxley and Waugh treat the confidence man in a self-consciously new light, their protagonists are more absurd than

those of recent novelists. Cary's allying the confidence man with
the artist moves him to a scene where "abnormalities" have long
been normal. Green carries the character into the servant class,
where again some cheating has been accepted—though his treatment of Middlewitch in *Back* suggests less enthusiasm for the
role in his own class. But the younger writers, heirs to a generation of approaching the confidence man obliquely, can treat him
as already almost normalized. Their heroes are not idiosyncratic,
but bright young men doing what they have been educated to
do. They accept as self-evident a difference between the social
role and absolute integrity, and, though they may dislike the gap,
do not find anywhere a strong disapproval of it. Society runs on
the contradiction.

The younger novelists also see that, though all the old motives
for the confidence role continue, social realities have tightened
and made escape to the next episode more like movement to an
identical situation. In responding doubly to the organization
world—wanting its rewards and disliking its standards—they
shift the center of reality from free play and self-expression to
the sterner game of career, where full freedom is impossible and
the question of what freedom and enjoyment remain is crucial.
In their writing the sensitive young man returns to the business
world from which he seceded around 1904, but he is still a rebel
—against opportunity.

The newer novelists recognize, too, how specialization limits
their confidence man's mobility. Since Joe Lampton has been
trained as an accountant, he cannot rapidly become a geologist.
Lucky Jim has studied to be a college history teacher and cannot readily become a stage designer. John Wain's Charles Lumley, the hero of *Hurry on Down*, has been educated to nothing—
he has a liberal arts degree—and finds that he can maintain
himself well only through the specialized trade of gag writer. In
such a society the hero not only finds it hard to better himself by
moving on, but can, by failing in the early stages, drop out of his
specialty altogether.

The real social theme of the "angry young men," then, is the
white-collar *fate*. Critics who emphasize the writers' class origins
are not wholly accurate even about these, and misread the novels

themselves, which summarize origins. The problem for the young man is not where he came from, but where he is going—and he is going to be civil servant, teacher, radio writer, or whatever. The sketched backgrounds of Lucky Jim and Joe Lampton serve as threats: the young man must make good in his specialty or suffer the work and living conditions of the lower classes. But, though the possibility helps keep the heroes running, they do not usually fail, and the white-collar rewards are real enough to give them reason for being of two minds about society's plans for them.

The younger novelists' sense of superiority to their predecessors rests most on the claim that their social situation is real to more people now than Huxley's and Waugh's. (Significantly, though the new heroes are more "normal," eccentricity still accretes in the organization itself.) Huxley recognizes briefly in the poverty scene that the problems of his coterie are special to the comfortable class, and in Waugh the outrageous confidence games automatically establish class distinction—only aristocrats could get away with them. The ability of his coterie to act foolishly with impunity is a badge of privilege.

In fact, the younger men write as if the stuffy office-goers whom Waugh means to outrage had suddenly become the chief novelists, with the view-from-down-here taken as reality. To them the confidence role is a bread-and-butter issue. Their threats are more direct, their anxiety founded in the social as well as the emotional world; Lucky Jim and Joe Lampton have no way to take off the false beard or run away to Azania. Yet for these later novelists, too, the confidence role appeals by its promise of a leap to prominence. Jim feels himself better qualified for director than functionary, but must use all his wits even to remain a functionary, and quick victory over the fuddy-duddies occurs only in the fairy-tale ending. But Joe does see a way, through marrying Susan, to leap over the years-in-grade progress of civil service, and Charles Lumley joins a group of dope smugglers to impress his girl that he is as arrived as her middle-aged guardian.

But, though Amis and Braine resist ready-made roles, they do not define sharply the integrity they are defending. For Joe

Lampton, it apparently means the right to love a woman who does not quite fit the social pattern and offers no economic promise. Like the loves of many outsiders, it thrives on negatives. Lucky Jim's integrity expresses itself mostly through his comments to himself on his superiors and his search for people of like mind—"ironic points of light"—in a false world. He finds his community outside the college—with the "ordinary chaps" at the boarding house, the girl from London, the agreeable aristocrat who rescues him.

However, John Wain, the most analytic mind among the younger writers, begins with an ideal of integrity in *Hurry on Down*—and sees it as the father of the confidence role. His hero has an education and a revulsion from the white-collar fate, but testing other ways convinces him that integrity does not follow automatically from becoming a Bohemian, a worker, or a secretary to a rich man. The Bohemian girl supports her writer by being mistress to an accountant; the honest workman and small businessman, Charles' associate in a window-washing business, goes to jail for trickery with automobiles and dope. As secretary to a rich man—Amis' magic solution—Charles finds himself responsible for the antics of the millionaire's relatives. As a hospital orderly, he cannot like the honest, uneducated girl whom an orderly should marry. The eternal feminine draws him, not onward and upward, but outward toward society and a millionaire's mistress. In the excellent throwaway ending, Wain shows him working as a radio gag man, fulfilling his promise—and selling it. Yet the tone suggests conciliation, for Charles accepts the paradox he would not accept at the beginning.

The younger novelists, then, take the inherited conflict expressed through the confidence man, and apply it to an up-to-date social report. Yet, once that report is in and initialed by the public, it seems complete, and the novelists have had difficulty in writing good second novels. In throwing off the old social analysis, they have not developed the psychological insight of two older writers. For all the excitement over the angry young men, L. P. Hartley and Anthony Powell have made the formidable new searches into personality and role.

CHAPTER EIGHT

Games of Apprehension

L. P. HARTLEY

No one shows spirit seeking collision with the given more unremittingly than L. P. Hartley. In England he is respected, but not popular. In America, few have read him and even fewer feel guilty about not having read him. Yet, along with Green and Powell, he changed the direction of the comic novel, raising even more seriously than they the question of whether it remains comic at all. Green brings the neurotic response to situations difficult for it to meet, but his cheer lets him find it handicapping rather than disabling. No one has shown with Hartley's detailed perception what happens when an established, inadequate emotional pattern leads its victim into circumstances where it will not work.

Hartley is a good writer and he should be read. My interest in him here begins at the point where his talent and his limitation meet, in his four novels of adult life. All four of these start from ingeniously different angles, and all four repeat a single dramatic tension. The real question about Hartley is not whether he is important enough to take seriously, but what continuing interest a writer can have who is at once so skillful and so rigid, so much, in Ben Hogan's phrase, "the captive of his own good stroke."

When Hartley first gained critical notice after the war with *Eustace and Hilda,* he was almost fifty and a well-known suspense story writer. A reader with enough prescience might have foreseen something about the novels in the several suspense stories where adults play hide-and-seek.

Hartley still sees human relations as absurdly dangerous games of hide-and-seek, though he no longer deals in mystery. His fresh-ness consists at first in simply changing the patterns of the naturalistic novel from social insights to emotional ones; yet in doing so he departs from both the older solid way of conceiving character and the more recent fluid way of conceiving conscious-ness. He sees character as a large psychological mechanism, work-ing through intricate smaller mechanisms that may seem uncon-nected, but never are. His talent, like the electronics technician's, is for starting with the large mechanism and tracing out all the interconnected, multicolored wires that together produce the major effect. His wires, though, are always connected; there are no short circuits or loose ends. And he is as confident as the technician that some of these mechanisms will sooner or later throw the machine out of order.

Eustace and Hilda, his longest novel (three volumes), is also his simplest version of character as repeated neurotic pattern. Eustace has already become accustomed at the age of eight or nine to being dominated by his sister Hilda, who is two years older. Throughout the long narrative he takes up opportunities to break the pattern, and always returns to it. Though Hartley documents the history relentlessly, he also creates highly in-dividual scenes—Eustace's running away with a girl playmate and his subsequent illness, his attraction and repulsion with old Miss Fothergill, his tense wait for Hilda's return from an airplane ride with a rival young man, his excitement in the fire-works scene at the Venice church, his pathetic attempt to sustain a sense of community by swimming in the Lido at dawn after the festival. Eustace's pro-and-con conversations with himself are a good technical innovation. But Hartley eschews action and variation almost as if he associated drama with potboiling.

In the adult novels Hartley works backward to combine this new talent for emotional mechanism with his old talent for con-flict and suspense. In the process he discovers the large mecha-nism that constitutes his major insight. "Beware of what you wish for in youth because you will get it in middle age," Stephen quotes Goethe in *Ulysses.* Hartley concentrates this dilemma into the comedy of a particular despair (second on Kierkegaard's list) —the wish to be someone else. More than most people, though, his characters cannot be anybody but themselves. They have worked to be exactly what they are, have made persistent efforts to fit in with some going ideal of conduct, and have established a clear social status. The timid writer, the suburban housewife, and the energetic social-worker seem, in the beginning, the commonest stereotypes, and mean to be just that. But a perverse desire to violate these carefully built images of themselves takes hold of them. They want, at the same time, a life so habitual as to create no emotional stress and a life different from the one they know how to live. Their intensity makes every reverse severe.

Hartley's main characters—angels all, in their fashion—try to balance on pin points which they have heretofore taken for solid platforms. They have a strong need for approval, a great fear of what other people will think, and a desire for significance by association with significant people. They are rigid and defensive, feeling threatened in themselves and in their environment. At twenty-eight, thirty-five, forty-nine—middle age comes earlier to some than to others—they are where they expected to be, and they want something more exciting. Kafka achieves a good deal of his horror by pulling the rug from under characters who hope they have achieved stability, but Hartley makes his hero kick the rug from under himself and go through the exciting, but frightening, effort to regain balance.

Hartley does not advocate these violations of type, rather distrusts them; but he takes them as the given of experience that his characters must work through as they can. Suppressed angers and wishes react upon people who habitually organize their emotions along with their activities. Since some suppression and organization are inevitable, Hartley easily leads the reader to hope throughout the novel that the outbreak he can see coming will after all not occur. The regular cycle of the novels moves from comedy to suspense, from slightly uncomfortable comfortableness to apprehension and a horrifying realization that the only possible direction is forward. Hartley shows the ideal of security leading to the same frenzy which, with Waugh, is the outcome of irresponsible rebellion.

All the main characters suffer from a common symptom:

though busy, they feel unemployed. Nothing that is both permissible and interesting turns up. Their desire for control over the strange and exciting takes the standard form of the misalliance. The timid bachelor falls in with the woman Communist, the suburban housewife with the Bohemian author, the social worker with the movie actor, the hard-boiled limousine driver with the neurotic society woman. Each main character involves himself in a romance which could work out only if he were extremely flexible—and, by definition, the Hartley hero is hardly flexible at all. Moreover, an unrecognized wish for power lies behind the impulse to break out of the secure restrictions. Characters who feel their areas of action unduly circumscribed deceive themselves into believing that they are helping someone else. The perfect woman is helping her husband's business, the writer is rowing "for the little children," and the social worker is trying to tame her husband for his own good.

Though Hartley repeats his larger mechanism through all the adult novels, his individuality shows even more in the minor mechanisms. The excellence of *The Boat* in this respect first made me think of him as an important writer. It is a mock-picaresque novel, with a hero full of schemes that he can only occasionally carry out. Though Hartley still emphasizes character as repeated neurotic pattern, this time he intertwines the episodes so skillfully that one difficulty remains unsettled while two or three others appear and disappear. The technique obliterates the straight-line effect of *Eustace and Hilda*.

The narrative moves unevenly through the Hartley cycle of minor frustration to sense of persecution to absurd outbreak. Timothy Casson, a bachelor of forty-nine, is at first too passive, then overaggressive, and finally, after his outbreak, too eager to retreat. He returns from Italy to the village of Upton-on-Swirrel at the beginning of the Second World War. After some years of living the sunny life and writing "pictures of Italy" for a British prestige magazine, he has adapted to the war by writing "pictures of England." He responds too much, though, to the necessary change by determining to make a general change in his way of life. He takes his accidental repatriation as the call to a planned rebirth and decides to become a member of the village gentry, a group of retired military men who fish and tend their lawns.

The determination to change, though, conflicts with a simple desire for recreation. He likes to scull and has bought an expensive boat. He soon learns that the Swirrel is a fishing river, legally restricted. The retired gentlemen say that rowing menaces the spawning of the fish.

"We do not get isolated, we choose it." Hartley shows Timothy making the choice over and over—in his efforts to join the gentry, his domestic establishment, his relations with his chosen intermediaries, his distaste for other newcomers, and his inability to hold the affection of women, children, and dogs. But the irritations do not appear in the orderly fashion of this list. They interwine so much that when Timothy finally lashes out at the "enemy," his vehemence is out of all proportion to his immediate problems. Again and again he has distorted his personality in an effort to please—and, just as he is on the verge of pleasing, has become angry and spoiled his chances.

The role of social suppliant apparently happens to Timothy because of the war, but he really creates the role. He wants to row *and* he wants to be accepted by people unlike himself. Part of the tension results from his passing up the several possible resolutions of the conflict between wish and status. Had he determined at once to row and be damned, the gentry might have accepted the *fait accompli,* as they do later. If he had wanted friends, the evacuees from London are eager to accept him. Rebellious acts from which he expects only disgrace make him a hero to his gardener, the local policeman, and the villagers, but he discounts their approval so long as the best people do not like him. He never asks himself whether he likes retired military men.

Also, he shows no faith in himself as a negotiator. He must have a social go-between, and chooses Mrs. Purbright, the rector's wife and the most impractical person in the community. She does arrange a tea for him to meet the best people, but Timothy fails his test by talking only to a young, blonde evacuee from London, whose chief topic is her hatred for the old residents.

Timothy's domestic arrangements introduce the first compounding of his problem. Unmarried, he has become dependent on his servants for companionship and affection. In Italy the service had been mildly inefficient, the affection great, but in England he can neither establish mastery nor make the servants all like him or get along with each other. Nothing less than perfect community will satisfy him. He tries at first to believe that the situation will work out. "At present I rely on the society of my servants," he writes a friend, "I think we are a happy nucleus."

But they are not. The cook not only "bellyaches" but is possessive about the passive parlormaid, who is not too secretly in love with the hearty gardener, who is married and has five children. The cook hates the gardener and, partly because she thinks he dislikes her, tries to get him in trouble with Timothy. The parlormaid likes Timothy, too, but the cook browbeats her into a common front. Knowing they are irreplaceable in wartime and counting on Timothy's domestic helplessness, they threaten regularly to give notice. Timothy, trying to placate the cook, alienates the gardener, his only sure friend.

Rejected and rejecting at home and abroad, he begins to suffer exaggerated fears, and finds grounds close at hand. The village policeman keeps his car in a shed on the property and, though actually a strong supporter of his "gentleman," intensifies Timothy's fear of the police. Resentment at the gentry, at Miss Chadwick, his lessor, and at the servants comes out in a fear of theft and property damage. And there are minor thefts and damage. A clothesbrush, an inkpot, a silver matchbox, and a snowstorm paperweight disappear. Timothy makes relations worse with the servants by questioning them. When Miss Chadwick turns out to have taken them for her own use, she merely says, "I couldn't very well steal my own property." Timothy protests about the inventory, but, as usual, allows her to browbeat him. "He still found great difficulty in making a nakedly hostile remark to anyone."

But the thefts that really worry Timothy are thefts of affection. Timothy has great fun with two small boys, evacuees from Birmingham, who come to live in his house, but the cook accuses the gardener of threatening to "skin 'em alive" and persuades their parents to steal them away. The apparent kidnaping is a real theft to Timothy.

His problems will not resolve themselves, though, as simple questions of enmity; he would actually be more comfortable if people would stay in the niches he has made for them. The cook conspires with the policeman and the other servants to get him a dog. He accepts the gesture of affection—partly because the rector has advised him that a dog will help win the confidence of the retired military men. Timothy comes to love the oversized hound, but even the villagers are afraid of him, and the cook wins away his affection by "cupboard love." Frustrated in the human and animal worlds, Timothy turns to the inanimate and tries to fall in love with an expensive bowl. The bowl is mysteriously broken, Timothy sees another attack, and his investigations again upset the household.

The subtler sections of *The Boat*, though, show Timothy trying to distort his personality for external ends and breaking out in anger at the distortion just as it is on the point of succeeding. He can endure being rejected, but cannot stand uncertain status. He gets along superbly with Captain Sturrock at a policemen's fund dinner. The captain promises to have him over at once and hints at discussing the boating situation. But the invitation does not come. Instead, just as Timothy finds the suspense unbearable, Captain Sturrock sends his hunting dogs to be quartered on Timothy's property, apparently in accordance with ancient custom. Timothy fights with the keeper and fires off a fighting note to Captain Sturrock. The mail crosses, he gets his invitation apologizing for the captain's bout with a cold, and can only send a hopeless apology.

The irritations of passivity develop into the irritations of this new and misdirected aggressiveness. He focuses a good deal of his hate on Mrs. Lampard, the chief landowner of the district, who could presumably make him acceptable by a word. Her daughter charms him, but when the daughter fails to keep her tacit bargain of getting him an invitation to her wedding, he writes an anonymous letter revealing that she and her fiancé are brother and sister. Mrs. Lampard goes insane. Timothy's curse has worked more effectively than he had imagined, and he has part of his "victory," for he can now tell himself that insanity and incest are at the heart of the established order.

His major aggression, though, comes out of his affair with the blonde young woman, which has all Hartley's distrust of the sexual relation. Vera Cross turns out to be the emissary of an old friend, a socialite who has run through a series of enthusiasms and ended in Communism. Vera's courtship of Timothy, for she takes the initiative, is part of a conspiracy to stir up anger against the local gentry. Her physical comings and goings—and, even more, her emotional ones—tease Timothy into still more violent anger and determine him to follow her in a mad exhibitionistic scheme to arouse his "natural allies," the people. Vera plans a well-advertised row down the river to the town bridge, where Timothy will address an assembly on the right to do what you want to do. He downs his doubts about Vera and the scheme by telling himself that he is at last beginning to control the situation instead of being dominated by it, though, almost simultaneously, he sees himself as an agent-provocateur drawing down other people's sins and aggressions on himself.

> That Vera was an awkward customer Timothy did not deny, but in wooing her he had wooed the world in all its variousness, had embraced its capacity to wound as well as its power to bless, and in winning her, making her his, he had been victorious not only over the world, but even his own suspiciousness of the world, his tendency to seek out only those elements and people who consorted with his temperament, and whom, by a forgivable but faulty logic he rated higher, morally higher, than the rest. Loving Vera was like loving nature . . . More mortifying still, he betrayed (to anyone who was interested) his good opinion of himself, for those he chose to honor possessed qualities like his own, and his praise of them, his complacency in calling them friends, was an indirect encomium of himself.

But he is reversing his temperament and the results, as with all such feats in Hartley, are disastrous.

The passage shows what Hartley's style at its best can do. The tone is reasonable, the apparent attitude toward the self realistic and modest. Articulateness worthy of a writer about exotic places balances itself prettily ("its capacity to wound as well as its power to bless"), expands its insight thoughtfully ("his own suspiciousness of the world, his tendency to seek out only those elements and people who consorted with his temperament"), and throws in the casual "by a forgivable but faulty logic." To a point the analysis of his temperament is accurate, but to Timothy the leap toward being someone else seems as realistic as the rest: "loving Vera was like loving nature." *If* it is, Timothy is no Wordsworthian.

Hartley can create this effect with so many variations that the issue continually seems new. His style becomes a rational, self-consciously literary mode of misunderstanding the irrational. His characters talk their way into believing in the new start which the tone shows is impossible.

From the time of Timothy's decision to row his denser frustrations disappear, and with them the major quality of the novel. The symbolic actions thereafter, though ingenious, become more mechanical. Timothy takes on the trip two boys from Birmingham, reincarnations of the evacuees, and the dog, another evidence of lost affection. Mrs. Purbright fights with Vera and throws her into the river to drown. The good, apparently weak mother overcomes the bad, apparently strong girl. A retired colonel, who has disregarded Timothy, helps rescue him when the boat goes over the falls, and joins in applauding his oarsmanship. Dangerous sport is on the verge of succeeding where tea and tact had failed. Two of Timothy's old friends reappear after his illness—illness regularly follows athletic activity in Hartley—and take over his problems. Esther will help to establish him in her own village for a while and Tyro will introduce him into war work, which Timothy has hitherto refused. Timothy agrees to participate in the country's war at last, but on his own terms.

His convalescence and gradual re-entry into society emphasize the tension illnesses which run through the novel. (Even Captain Sturrock's cold has humorous significance.) Mrs. Purbright's husband and friends think of her as emotionally frail; Mrs. Lampard becomes actually ill; Edgel Purbright returns from the war with ulcers; Magda, who has regularly visited sanitariums, dies in one; and Timothy suffers from paranoid tendencies long before the boat trip. All these illnesses have in common an inability to face the demands of the day. Mrs. Purbright suffers from nostalgia for Edwardian times and constantly recommends retreat to Timothy; Mrs. Lampard suffers because she has been unwilling to face the truth about her past; Edgel dislikes the service and wants to write; Magda turns from boredom to hatred of her old friends; and Timothy, the avatar of this illness, cannot deal with his aggressions on a day-to-day basis or face his prospects realistically. He tries to deny the existence of the war, tries to become a lover at fifty after not having been one in his youth, and tries to break into a settled group with interests totally opposed to his.

But why did he fix on rowing? Esther and Tyro ask each other this question and Tyro gives an offhand answer, "A death wish." The answer doubtless applies to the actual rowing over "the devil's staircase" during a flood, but the fixation on the boat develops by attaching a series of conflicts to itself.

The boat has both social and sexual suggestion. At first Timothy thinks of his forthcoming trip as "the psycho-physical sensations that [he] would capture with the first free stroke of his free sculls in the free water: the release, the renewal." As his difficulties multiply, his wish for freedom from inhibition and inactivity takes on a religious tone. Later, when prospects are better, he sees rowing as the sign of his coming acceptance into the community. Then, frustrated again, he falls into Mrs. Purbright's scheme and begins to enjoy the pleasures of sacrifice. He decides to immolate the boat on a public pyre, again with appropriate speeches about reconciliation. When this idea proves impracticable he tries a substitute pleasure, renting a boat in town, but falls into an absurd feud with the crew of a train which runs along the bank. Finally, the rowdiness of soldiers and young people forces the closing of the rental agency and Timothy once more has to face the issue of rowing his own boat.

The boat is a still more flexible symbol later. Excited by the approaching marriage, Timothy visits the boat in the boathouse and sees it as a rusty Sleeping Beauty, ready to be roused at his touch. In his most regressive mood, he believes he is making his row "for the children," who will afterward be free to do as they please. And, as he begins the trip, he sees the boat as a throne and himself as an emperor. A little later he mythologizes his situation with himself as Jason and the rowboat as the *Argo*. The boat records his emotional shifts through the novel, from the wish for "release, renewal" to the exhibitionism of flying the hammer and sickle.

The Boat, then, comes nearer than any other novel to developing the range of Hartley's themes. It sets up the conflict between love and status, and shows love as an inviting betrayal, status as a will-o'-the-wisp. It works out—in Mrs. Purbright, Mrs. Lampard, Esther, and Miss Chadwick—a composite picture of older women as supporters and arbitrary authority. The potential fathers are unapproachable.

Most important, *The Boat* isolates the qualities of the Hartley hero. Oversensitive, uncomfortable with people unlike himself, fearful of disregard and desertion, outwardly eager to please and angry at the distortions of his personality he believes necessary to please, he feels awkward, incapable of coping with his own emotions and day-to-day relations with people. He consequently searches for some great action which will overcome his own low estimate of himself—which he takes to be also other people's estimate. Hartley's heroes live in a world of continual failure and continual effort to regroup.

These heroes end in understandable retreat, which Hartley takes as inevitable. Each novel ends with a period of convalescence and a move toward some harbor where the previous troubles will not recur—back home in *Eustace and Hilda,* back to the suburbs in *A Perfect Woman,* to "facts" in *The Go-Between,* to the church in *My Fellow Devils,* and to Esther and Tyro in *The Boat.* Hartley holds out no hope that his characters can ever understand their difficulties and return to deal effectively with their problems. Instead, he gives them a minimum of insight while retaining for himself a maximum insight into the course of their crises. He concludes with a desire for peace. He does not, of course, specify success in finding this refuge, but he takes the wish for it as the ultimate wisdom of experience. His characters abandon the excitement of the new and strange to search for some niche where they can exist on a minimum of animal faith.

I have discussed *The Boat* at length because, more than any other novel, it shows Hartley's comic range. His later adult novels develop less than most writers', but important changes occur. Timothy has both eccentricity and the desire to belong. In the later novels, Hartley splits these qualities. The main character becomes so thoroughly his stereotype that he no longer has visible eccentricities. But, significantly, he is attracted to people whose instability seems their greatest appeal and their most effective defense. The main characters fall in with experts at absorbing "help" without giving anything in return. The device enables Hartley to treat both sides sympathetically and to avoid the more abstract antagonists of *The Boat*. More important, the shift brings into the open his central conflict between the stereotyped and the neurotic. The neurotic attracts the stereotype like the lost half of the famous egg.

As in all Hartley's novels, the main character in *My Fellow Devils* enters upon the quest for control of the strange and exciting almost as a game. Margaret Pennyfeather, a social worker and justice of the peace in her suburban community, takes up with a tough-guy movie star as an adventure so outlandish that nothing can be expected from it. When something does come of it, she tries to appeal to, and twist her personality toward, the vagaries of the artist. But one vagary is too much for her: her new husband goes in for burglary, even burglary of their own apartment. The tensions in the novel follow from Margaret's efforts to accommodate a changing view of her public hero become private villain, her failure, and her strain in rallying to a common front when there is no understanding and no common value.

But *My Fellow Devils* dramatizes the Hartley conflict as none of the other novels do; in it he at last succeeds in creating an appealing, rounded antagonist. For all her individuality in action, Margaret is obviously the familiar character who has earned her stereotype and wants something more exciting. As a type, Colum, her husband and devil, is new to Hartley's novels, though not to contemporary comic fiction: he is the anxious confidence man who so often appears as the "normal" hero. Here, however, he represents a threat to the human rather than an adaptation to it. His chameleon attractiveness, which makes him the Tempter, comes from his ability to impose himself upon the movie public in so many dominating roles. All of Hartley's protagonists—Eustace, Timothy, the perfect wife, the limousine driver in *The Hireling*—resent their choices and the necessity of living with them; the chameleon Colum does not. Limitation is Hartley's norm of the human condition, but Colum is the devil because he holds out the lure that attractive change is natural. He has no center and seems never to need one; his emotional ups and downs are no more than barometers of external events. Though he finds it hard to change from gangster to gentleman blackmailer, he can do it—superbly. Margaret can be only what she has been. Colum is a talented illusionist who leads on to illusion people who cannot bear it.

Modern comic fiction, though, brings real emotions into the rogue character; in fact, it is almost true that the confidence man's grounds for anxiety define his individuality. Far from being the perfect rogue who imposes upon other people and goes free himself, Colum is anxious about his own reality. He can convey the illusion of toughness and criminality. Is he actually tough and clever enough to commit crime and outwit pursuit? His burglaries act out this wish to test himself, to pit himself against the respectable society represented by Margaret—and the police. His burglaries outwit the police, but not Margaret, who tries to adapt to them as a fact and to help him. The question then becomes, at what point will his recklessness draw the line? Ironically, when Colum does finally hesitate, the police arrest him at once. (He has planned to participate in a mock holdup of an older woman friend; the woman dies of a heart attack, and everyone believes Colum to be involved.) Margaret, frightened by the burglaries, believes him capable of the crime and therefore guilty. Once he escapes punishment, though, he becomes his nonself again.

Hartley also reverses the previous proportions between his mixed genres. In *The Boat*, comedy predominates and suspense takes over only near the end; in *My Fellow Devils*, suspense appears early and continues. The comedy, almost all at Margaret's expense, comes from her struggle to control the reeling situation and occurs while she seems to be controlling it.

> It was long past getting-up time but she read the letter again, and in the light of her softened feeling for Colum a new interpretation came to her that, in a fit of hysteria, she had put a totally false construction on an innocent, commonplace transaction, perhaps it was not meant to bamboozle her at all. Perhaps it was—well, a tacit admission of guilt, so framed as to leave the way open to understanding and forgiveness; a face-saving letter, both for Colum and her. She had caught him out, yes; but the letter took it for granted that she still loved him; and the charges of hysteria and loss of mental balance, the false account of what had happened—they were not impudent attempts to confute an enemy, a prosecuting counsel, they were offered to her as to someone who loved him, and who would grasp eagerly at the opportunity—not to think better of him, but to preserve his good name in the eyes of the world. She could not, how could she? expect him to confess in so many words that he was a wrong 'un; but he could provide her with a loophole large enough to admit both her knowledge and her love.
> 'Do this for me,' the letter now seemed to say. 'Pretend for my sake that you have made a mistake.'

As in *The Boat*, Hartley's comedy here derives from the all but impeccable reasoning used to misunderstand reality. Unlike many comic writers, he deals with characters whose education and intelligence approximate his own and who make their mistakes through pride in mind, a belief that they are objectively estimating a situation when in fact they are misconstruing their own and others' emotions. In the brief passage Hartley insinuates the balancing of absolutes that finally lead Margaret to look for refuge in religion. The angry "bamboozle" strikes against "totally false construction of an innocent, commonplace transaction;" "charges of hysteria and loss of mental balance, the false account" against "admission of guilt," "face-saving," "loophole;" "enemy, a prosecuting counsel" against "understanding and forgiveness," "someone who loved him." But this absolute mode of thinking omits two facts. Colum does not mean what he says in the letter, and Margaret does not understand the will to punish behind her "understanding and forgiveness." Her incomprehension provides the next comic turn:

> No other disinfectant would be needed. Colum's letter amounted to a confession; and in the circumstances, confession must also mean repentance and a determination to amend. What else could it mean? It would not be easy for him, at first, to live with her, knowing that she knew about him; it would be a daily mortification and she would have to lighten the burden of it. She would be the most considerate of policewomen, but a policewoman she would be, her presence and her knowledge his safeguard against further lapses. That would be his punishment—if she could think of punishment in connection with him—to be always within sight of the one person who knew his secret but would never tell it, not even to her father, least of all to him.
>
> Unconsciously, but not unwillingly, Margaret began to think of herself as a kind of celestial blackmailer, levying on Colum a perpetual tribute of good behaviour, perhaps, more positively, of good works, a servitude he would gladly undergo since it would be sweetened on both sides by love.
>
> But would love be enough? Ought Colum to go through some decontamination process? He had written (no doubt facetiously) of a psychiatrist for her; why not a psychiatrist for him?

Hartley builds around burglary one of the defter treatments of the sexual struggle. The slight authorial intrusions—"unconsciously, but not unwillingly," "celestial blackmailer"—provide a metaphorical comic perspective.

The suspense grows as Margaret and the reader realize that she is not succeeding, that Colum is too self-willed and emotional ever to respond to any "adjustment" of hers. The suspense depends, though, on the same will to a delusion of power that the comedy does. But in the suspense scenes the reader has lost faith in the possibility of dealing with the situation, while Margaret drives herself to believe that she can adapt, can change her husband from the delinquent he is and portrays so effectively. Her diary shows rhythmic shifts from rejection to new effort:

> 'I'm not being hard on you,' I said.
> . . . Suddenly I felt shy and humble, in the presence of his abasement.

But Margaret cannot really believe in these abasements, and the next chapter opens with doubt forcing itself upon her, "But Margaret's dream of partnership was shattered by a dream. It was dark. . . ."

In both *The Boat* and *My Fellow Devils* Hartley's mixture of genres has its own consistency: situations are shown "under the aspect of comedy" as long as the possibility of control exists; the sense of experience as prolonged crisis begins when the probability of not controlling overrides the faith in management. In Sartre's view, anguish arises from free choice, from the constant possibility of voluntarily not doing what the situation demands. In Hartley's novels, unbearable suspense—anguish—arises from a fear of not having the emotional strength to deal with a situation that defies all rational effort. Margaret makes continuing "free" choices which only make the problem worse.

Even while Margaret asserts to herself most strongly that love and kindness will cure the delinquency that she cannot understand, Hartley lays the groundwork for her desire to withdraw from the situation. The religious sanction for the wish is planted almost too carefully. Halfway through, Father McBane shocks Margaret by advising her to separate from Colum. Though she believes that she wants to become a Catholic for her husband's sake, Father McBane says that she wants to for her own sense of security. For months she has been seeking "peace of mind"— Hartley uses the phrase—and practical help, like the return of stolen objects, from St. Anthony. Unlike her rational plans, this irrational impulse to "church-crawling" works. She gets back the stolen objects, at the price of losing faith in Colum, and she does gain a temporary peace. Near the end of the novel, with the common front irreparably broken, she tries a last "rational" plan—going back to the lawyer she had thrown over for Colum. When this fails, she turns wholeheartedly to the Church. Even here Hartley does not permit a straightforward solution, but uses the religious urgency to heighten Margaret's sense of need. The local priest, less subtle than Father McBane, counsels a return to her husband and ends believing sadly that she should have been a nun. But, as with Timothy and the war, Margaret drives toward her goal of religious satisfaction on her own terms, and the novel concludes with her breaking into a run on the way to her first, almost clandestine, communion.

The neurotic writer in *The Boat* tries to adapt to the stereotypes around him; Margaret strains to please the artist of neurosis. Statistically, at least, Hartley has found this last symbolic action more meaningful—and perhaps more cheering. Both of his other adult novels follow it. *A Perfect Woman,* the most straightforward comedy of the four, raises a new prospect: recognition of the impossible may make for living with the possible. As usual, the main character suffers from the delusion of infinitely transformable personality. A restless, intelligent suburban housewife invites a novelist to her club as a gambit to outfox the previous program chairmen. She outfoxes them and herself. She falls in love with the novelist, but he prefers a fresh young refugee barmaid. The barmaid in turn likes the housewife's husband, prefers stability to genius, but has already involved herself with another young refugee. Out of these complications, the Hartley suspense appears to indicate the impossibility and painfulness of the whole mixed program. And out of the impossibility the housewife and her husband return happily to their stereotypes, a little better satisfied for their adventures with the strange and dangerous.

The Hireling streamlines and brings further into the open the conflict of neurosis and stereotype. The driver of a for-hire limousine—unmarried, a retired sergeant—has built his life on punctuality, orderliness, impersonality, and a drive for power. To fit into the demands of a nervous, but rich young woman, a client, he begins the game of painting for her a fantasy picture of his stable, ordinary home life with a wife and children. But what he considers a deception good for business turns out to be his own fantasy of the good life. He helps his client recover from her "nervous breakdown," but becomes lost himself and dreams of the impossible home life he has imagined—with the rich young woman. The neurotic temperament shows unexpected resiliency and the apparently stable, inhibited man founders against it.

At the moment Hartley needs interpretation more than reservation, but it should be safe now to say a word about his limita-

tions. Esthetically, they are the obverse of his talents: he knows
the inside of the tidy temperament, and has a good deal of it
himself. His disorders are very orderly, progress smoothly to
determined conclusions. He takes so much interest in defeat that
he sometimes seems to impose it on his characters. As with the
religious motif in *My Fellow Devils,* he plants his suspense.
Morally, Hartley represents the old alliance of the mechanist
with passivity. For my taste he is too committed to a quietist
ideal. He shows peace of mind disturbed, then regaind after
frenzy. If he were a little less grey in tone and a great deal less
sensitive in style, he might have been a popular author, for in
other forms peace of mind has done well indeed.

But Hartley has marked off an area of comedy and terror that
is his own and he handles it with great skill. Behind each of his
major characters stands an image, never quite revealed, of a
character with godlike power to impose himself on others and
remain invulnerable to the stresses they give rise to. Such a
character would transcend the limits of his own personality,
know his direction without having to learn it, and magically
dissolve the intractableness of other people's natures. Because
Hartley's characters take this image as their real selves, they are
in despair and seek refuge from further experience. Hartley
brings up to date the view of people as faulty mechanisms too
weak to stand the process of growth, yet unable to accept stasis.
Henry Green often uses growth as a standard for his characters;
Hartley usually sees it as an unmanageable necessity. The use of
stereotypes for defense does not produce security, but only a
need for renewed contact with the strange and disorderly; but
people are animals too highly specialized to transform themselves much. Human relations are a continuing, voluntary game
of hide-and-seek, with great risks and few prospects of finding.
Hartley is more sensitive than any of his contemporaries to the
fearful will to failure that accompanies all confidence.

CHAPTER NINE

The Uses of Polite Surprise

ANTHONY POWELL

IN THE THIRTIES Anthony Powell was the perennial junior executive of the British novel, always effective, always on the verge of great things, yet always with his name on the same door. If his postwar series, *The Music of Time,* has at last made him a major writer, it still suggests long hours and hard work more than the offhand brilliance of early Waugh or early Huxley. His mannered, depressed, analytical style does more than any other around—always excepting Ivy Compton-Burnett's—to put the reader off. For a long time, too, Powell gives no ground to the reader who wants the story to go somewhere; when it does, the winding, weighing-the-evidence voice of the narrator goes on unchanged. It has now gone unchanged through six volumes.

Nevertheless, *The Music of Time* is gaining readers and critical attention. Arthur Mizener's article* establishes its importance and describes its tone and scope. My purpose is to look at the *where* of its comedy—specifically, at the dramatic conflicts and the underlying sense of character and society.

For over half a century depth psychologies have been exploring the collision between the demands of the present and patterns fixed in the individual past, and within recent years this knowledge has become so widely accepted that a contemporary novelist need neither explain nor justify it. (A question-and-answer column in the morning newspaper provides summaries for the emotional proletariat.) This understanding raises a new set of problems which novelists have been slow to explore. A person who understands his emotional patterns and their devel-

---

* See Bibliography, p. 170 below.

opment does not respond to new situations as he "naturally" would. (What "naturally" means can best be seen in Hartley, whose characters repeat neurotic patterns until these become inadequate enough to cause outbreaks. Hartley, however, keeps his understanding to himself as author and denies most of it to his characters.) Powell is the only comic novelist to give his narrator and central figure the awareness to face further experience in the light of these patterns from the past. He has, in fact, been so orthodox that he is unorthodox.

In spite of this clear originality, Powell seems dogged by the question of literary indebtedness, and facing this directly is probably the quickest means of defining his individuality. He seems fated to be praised as like someone else: in the thirties it was Waugh, now it is Proust. Unquestionably, the narrator's voice in *The Music of Time* does have an echo, but the significance of the fact is generally misunderstood. For forty years critics have been saying that modern literature, having broken with the past, has lost the benefits of a solid tradition; the novelists have been the first to discover that the famous break has by now become a tradition of its own. Green, Hartley, Cary, and Powell all build on respectable modern classics without in any serious way resembling them. They write like the scholar who, confronted with the formidable set of cruxes in Shakespeare or Donne, chooses to raise another sort of question and stake out the space as work in progress. Powell does use a vaguely Proustian framework, but with a new set of cruxes. The best of his early work was not like Waugh and none of his later work is really like Proust.

But he was of Waugh's world and the world just before Waugh. The conflicts in *The Music of Time* develop out of the rebellions in the first quarter of the century. The novel uses a central image of the twenties and thirties, party-going, and may be the last significant novel about it that we shall have for a while, since the focus of fictional reality has shifted. In its day the image developed considerable variety, but its core remained a test of rebellious fun carried on in style. As has been said, even in Huxley's loose associations of rebels, characters recreate from the remoter past—Lypiatt as Michelangelo, Mercaptan as Crébillon the Younger, Coleman as the Slavic Satanist, Rosie as the Great Lady, Shearwater as the earnest Victorian scientist. They justify their rebellion against the present by trying to live myths. Waugh, with his tight coteries, puts the issue of identity squarely as a choice of existing styles, an effort to absorb miseries and hope to an available manner.

Exactly this choice seems to confront the narrator, Nick Jenkins, in *A Buyer's Market* (second in the series), but for Powell now the issue is a false one. Though Nick does not know it, he has hostages in all camps—the world of power, the correct social world, the fast set, and the Bohemian. And not only Nick. All his friends struggle through difficulties caused by their inability to stylize themselves. The cumulative detail of the novel documents a paradox between faith and fact: people believe in groups and must be individuals. And the motive for Powell's documentation parallels the motive of earlier twentieth-century novelists who felt themselves fighting an established image of mind and character. For Powell the mind is neither the rationalist rogue planning to get its way as best it can, as it often is for Waugh, nor the tireless collector of symbols around obsessions, as it is for Joyce and Green. It is instead a collector and manufacturer of categories, of tags to fit every person and occasion. Upbringing establishes the first categories in the young mind, and experience becomes a baffling effort to make these rough and ready labels fit a mixed reality.

Powell takes his framework from Proust because Proust is the serious student of the party-going that Huxley and Waugh see as obvious and immediate. They test a going faith. Proust and Powell research into a faith once held and, like historians of all lost causes, ask at many points what went wrong. No one else has developed so elaborate an apparatus as Proust for such an investigation; yet the differences are more significant. Powell never abandons the present for the past, as he did in an early novel like *Venusberg* and as Proust does systematically. Since understanding and the passage of time do not change a man's emotional nature, nostalgia doubtless enters into Powell's revisiting the twenties and thirties, but the later novel sees nostalgia as more a disease than a design for living. More important, Proust has no utilitarian motive in his research; Powell clearly believes that understanding the "dance of time" makes the present more livable.

The structure of the novel resembles Proust's formidable *recherche* for time lost primarily in its inclusive detail; Nick has little of Marcel's form-by-association. He tells a chronological story, shifting to different locales and characters but seldom backward and forward in time. Time moves onward as persistently in Nick's story as in Arnold Bennett, and the changes it brings, rather than the possibility of reliving lost experience, interest him.

For Nick is not trying to recapture the past; *The Music of Time* is hardly a novel of sensibility at all. Powell does not want, like Joyce, Proust, Virginia Woolf, and most of the first-generation novelists of the century, to capture the quiver of the nerves, "as if a magic lantern. . . ." He tries instead to understand, to look hard at motives and consequences in people dealing with realities which they must deal with whatever their inner refinements. This sense that life continues, that problems go on arising in old but unexpected ways, distinguishes Powell sharply from the Proustian sense of the past as the main repository of meaning. For Powell, the past is little more than an accessible view of the present, never a mystique. Where Proust's style is often warm and excitable, Powell's is invariably cool. The essence of *understanding* the past—and indirectly the present and future—is loss of the particular excitements, angers, and hopes that give the present its complexity and incomprehensibility. Powell wants to clarify, not to relive.

In Proust, again, the social movement shows the replacement of the better by the worse. The driving bourgeoisie penetrate the aristocracy and destroy the old alliance between esthete and aristocrat. Powell also shows what looks like the defeat of the better by the worse, but the observed fact moves him to stress "what looked like" and reopen the question of value. Was there a weakness in Stringham's attitudes and a strength in Widmerpool's that escaped Nick in school? That kind of question is never closed.

Moreover, Nick has no nostalgia for a fading aristocracy. He sees Britain in the late twenties as already commercial through and through, with business the accepted road to power and titles. Proust's aristocrats are nobility without portfolio, without function beyond maintaining manners for a limited society. Nick sees only sad, unglamorous, if friendly, futility in the country gentleman forcibly retired from diplomacy or the over-age general clinging to a ceremonial court post. All the world is bourgeois—artists, writers, gentlemen perhaps most of all—or passé. That battle cannot be refought.

Since the insights that Powell exploits have been developing in literature for a long time, he can treat them as familiars. Nick's main qualification as a hero is a will to flexibility. Polite surprise is not only his manner, but his way of meeting reality, a therapeutic principle for dealing with reversals. His determination to keep in contact with the present gives him both his tone of voice and his claim on the reader's confidence. And the tone of polite surprise, pervasive and persuasive as it is, creates an action that can never quite complete itself. For all its apparent slowness *The Music of Time* centers on action and develops its characters—even its eccentrics—more as Nick's response to them than as independent entities. This action sets up a continuing conflict between expectations and experiences, the winter book odds and the actual race. Being alive means meeting, half resentfully, half interestedly, the challenge of change without losing continuity and direction. Experience will enter into no contract with the vague road markers set up by childhood and youth. The adult must keep the complicated, interesting, irritating present in some relation to the formulae from the past. Hopefully, distaste for the present and future will not produce either a frenzy for new experiences or a retreating regard for the past that will overwhelm the personality. Whereas for Hartley life is an alternating current of frenzy and retreat, a recurring traumatic shock, for Powell it is a series of small shocks to be met with slightly raised eyebrows and the instantaneous question of how it all fits. Above everything else, Nick wants to know within a safe margin of error where he is at any given moment.

For another thing, Nick's small shocks are the more bearable because they seem to be happening to somebody else. He has the gift of being in the game and out of it at the same time. He goes to school, works, goes to parties, has a love affair, gets married, all with the air of a man whose own doings do not quite bear on the central problems of experience or this novel. He lives by keeping track of others, not as they affect his plans, but as barometers of how things are going at this stage of life. If these others mirror his own inner reality—and they must—what goes on in the mirror is so much more interesting and comprehensible than what happens to Nick that he seems to go through life absent-mindedly, managing his own affairs with his left hand.

His secret is listening, which serves as both connection and forecast. From the first he is passive, receptive to experience but uninclined to pursue it, convinced that the right things will happen of themselves at the proper time. His own experience thus lags behind his more active contemporaries'; when he comes to make a living, go to parties, or have a love affair, he already has an encyclopedia of others' difficulties. This bent accounts for the raised eyebrows instead of indignation: he knows better than any of his friends that whatever happens has happened before. He has faith in his friends' defeats—and dislikes the kind of person who wins. So he enters his affair with Jean Templer resigned to her leaving him presently. He appears unworried by his slow start as a writer and an editor of art books, but feels sadness at similar checks to other people. His forewarned nature prevents his making outlandish mistakes, though outlandish mistakes occur all around him.

A Question of Upbringing and *A Buyer's Market* deal with the choices of youth, *The Acceptance World* and *At Lady Molly's* with their wearing quality. *A Question of Upbringing* shows schoolboys choosing up sides for the pull ahead, though, since everything *is* a "question of upbringing," Nick makes no conscious choice at all. In his threesome of bright, prankish, but lazy boys, Stringham is the brilliant ironist, Peter Templer the specialist in girls, and Jenkins the follower of both. Stringham and Templer come from families active in "the City," Nick from a military family, a fact which may account for his strong sense of hierarchy. The boys live luxuriously, do much as they please, and make life hard for the housemaster. Life shapes up for them as a contest, hardly a race, between the fast boys and the mudders.

Nick observes later that some people seem destined to accompany each other through life, and the bright boys find their antagonist at once in Widmerpool, a born mudder. Every day in the drizzly fall weather the boys watch by the fireplace while Widmerpool jogs along in a track suit. He runs awkwardly, never improves, finishes last or next to last in every race, but keeps jogging. As the novel progresses, this jogging becomes more and more amazing—and disquieting—to the three naturals. What is shaping up is the division Mizener refers to between men of imagination and style and men of power. The stylists will say the brilliant things, maintain effortless decorum, and drift or feel they are drifting even when getting along fairly well; the men of power will talk dully, plan confidently, act awkwardly, and run the world. But Nick's is not a world well lost for style, and his sadness begins, like Waugh's heroes', in the triumph of the apparently inhuman over the human. (This conflict of natural and earned merit echoes a persistent conflict in nineteenth-century fiction, but few earlier novelists so wholeheartedly side with grace against good works.)

The conscious choices begin in *A Buyer's Market.* The supposed goods of the world fail to inspire a sustained enthusiasm in Nick. All is for sale, the buyer waits. A cheerless review of party-going that should have provided community fun and did not gives the novel its pervading depression. The question of *why not?* hangs over everything. In the dirigible party in Waugh's *Vile Bodies,* no one is having much fun, but the style conveys a vigorous effort. Equally outrageous acts occur in *A Buyer's Market,* but in a style so benumbing that everything seems to happen in slow motion. At a correct party Widmerpool, the mudder, grasps his girl's wrist as she tries to leave for another table:

> If she had been in a calmer mood, Barbara would probably, in the light of subsequent information supplied on the subject, have paid more attention to the strength, and apparent seriousness, of Widmerpool's feelings at that moment. As it was, she merely said: "Why are you so sour tonight? You need some sweetening."

She turned to the sideboard that stood by our table, upon which plates, dishes, decanters, and bottles had been placed out of the way before removal. Among this residue stood an enormous sugar castor topped by a heavy silver nozzle. Barbara must have suddenly conceived the idea of sprinkling a few grains of this sugar over Widmerpool as if in literal application of her theory that he "needed sweetening," because she picked up this receptacle and shook it over him. For some reason, perhaps because it was so full, no sugar at first sprayed out. Barbara now tipped the castor so that it was poised vertically over Widmerpool's head, holding it there like the sword of Damocles above the tyrant. However, unlike the merely minatory quiescence of that normally inactive weapon, a state of dispensation was not in this case maintained, and suddenly, without the slightest warning, the massive silver apex of the castor dropped from its base, as if severed by the slash of some invisible machinery, and crashed heavily to the floor: the sugar pouring out on to Widmerpool's head in a dense and overwhelming cascade.

More from surprise than because she wished additionally to torment him, Barbara did not remove her hand before the whole contents of the vessel—which voided itself in an instant of time— had descended upon his head and shoulders, covering him with sugar more completely than might have been thought possible in so brief a space. . . .

Barbara was, without doubt, dismayed by the consequences of what she had done; not, I think, because she cared in the least about covering Widmerpool with sugar, an occurrence, however deplorable, that was hard to regard, with the best will in the world, as anything other than funny at that moment. This was the kind of incident, however, to get a girl a bad name; a reputation for horseplay having, naturally, a detrimental effect on invitations.

(When I first read Powell, I thought a successful novel could not be written in sentences like these, but presently the style seemed so accurate a projector for the slow-motion rerun of the past that I no longer noticed it at all.)

The structure of the novel surveys possibilities via three long parties—a correct dinner dance for bringing the young together, a fast set party, and a Bohemian birthday party for an elderly painter. Nick turns up none of these possibilities himself. They all come through family or school influence. He goes to the correct dinner dance because he is an eligible bachelor of proper background; to the fast set party because Stringham, now very fast indeed, takes him; and to the Bohemian party because the painter has been a family friend. In which group does he belong? He never states his question, but implicitly he tries to find a tailored identity through a choice of associates.

As usual, though, in Powell, experience will not fit the categorical form of the question. If it has an answer, the answer is that for different reasons he belongs in all three groups. Typically, though, he notices first that other people take their parties mixed and, more surprising, that they violate his type characterizations of them with impunity. Widmerpool, whose awkwardness should disqualify him as a suitable bachelor, appears at the correct dinner dance and acts as if he has both the habit and the right. He tags along to the fast-set party, falls in with the Bohemian Gipsy Jones, and presently has an affair with her. To Nick he is a grotesque, objectifying Nick's fear of awkwardness in situations where manner is all, but his success in "the City" makes it impossible for Nick to impose the old-school view on others.

The correct party, with its chaperons and carefully matched young people, evolves by apparent accident into the smart party, where manners are freer, the men and women have been matched off over and over, the hostess with the Greek name has been the mistress of a prince. She likes diversity of cast. Here the men of power and the men of imagination meet on presumably neutral ground, though the young beauties gravitate to the men of power. A rising financier, a Balkan prince, and Nick's hyperactive college adviser meet here, along with Widmerpool, the Bohemian painter Mr. Deacon, and his consort Gipsy. Nick sees all this as more exciting, even for a spectator, than the correct world he is expected to fit into, but the party ends in Mr. Deacon's hysterical outburst at the hostess and a meeting with Uncle Giles, the family misanthrope.

The third section moves to the countryside for two views of the world of power. As a guest in the country house of an ex-diplomat, forcibly retired for a forgotten blunder in a forgotten country, Nick sees power in decline. Here correct form appears as a defense against confusion and indecisiveness about what next—Nick's own problems. The family decides to visit the restored castle of a rising financier, a representative of the new power. With the ex-diplomat indecisiveness has become professional but remains real:

"It is all very perfect now," said Sir Gavin. "Rather too perfect for my taste. In any case, I am no medievalist."

He looked round the table challengingly after saying this, rather as Uncle Giles was inclined to glare about him after making some more or less tendentious statement, whether because he suspected that one or the other of us, in spite of this disavowal, would charge him with covert medievalism, or in momentary hesitation that, in taking so high a line on the subject of an era at once protracted and diversified, he ran risk of exposure to the impeachment of "missing something" thereby, was uncertain.

At the castle Nick sees the difference between power and imagination dramatized in Sir Magnus, the financier. By Nick's touchstone of brilliant talk, Sir Magnus comes out a zero, but he is clearly not a zero:

Sir Magnus himself did not talk much, save intermittently to express some general opinion, which, when during a comparative silence his words were wafted to the farther end of the table, on the lips of a lesser man would have suggested processes of thought of a banality so painful—of such profound and arid depths, in which neither humor, nor imagination, nor, indeed, any form of human understanding could be thought to play the smallest part—that I almost supposed him to be speaking ironically, or teasing his guests by acting the part of a bore in a drawing-room comedy.

But when Sir Magnus takes the guests on a tour of the dungeons and talks playfully of chaining the ladies there, he is frightening. People who run the world have the oddities of will, imaginative people have the oddities of imagination, Nick concludes, but the equation never completes itself to make these oddities equal the same thing.

Nick does not join the world of power, interesting as it is to him, though he later moves easily in the smart set. The immediate possibility for him is the Bohemian, where manners are even freer and access easier. This world, however, represents the contradiction of categories at its height. The artists, writers, and social theorists, apparently in revolt against the centers of power, struggle for power more bitterly and openly than the businessmen. The women are slumming aristocrats or untidy copies of the young women at the correct dinner dance. A rugged young Marxist critic and a less rugged Freudian critic scheme to control and use an established older writer. Gipsy Jones, the female deity of the cult, who distributes *War Never Pays* and a sort of affection, turns out to be the low form of the same girl of which Barbara Goring is the high type—energetic, noisy, uninhibited, self-willed. Nick is not consoled to find that he and Widmerpool have the same high and low tastes.

The "choice" of an identity through leisure activity seems to Nick the central problem at this stage of life, but a deeper conflict begins to appear. Nick is trying to down the awkward. Though the fear is his own, it takes the form of an obsession about Widmerpool. Both are in love with Barbara, both have a try at the smart set and end with Gipsy Jones, both are starting careers—Widmerpool with direction and success, Nick more uncertainly. The last scene of the novel shows them having dinner, family style, with Widmerpool's mother.

Widmerpool is not a freak accidentally successful, and awkwardness is not mere lack of gracefulness. His awkwardness is, for Nick, at the heart of the will to control events, which can never have the precision possible in the static study of human nature. Control does not lend itself to definition and speculation, but to choices which can go wrong. As the novel progresses, this awkwardness associates itself with several characters who are making a strenuous effort to will the future. Its opposite, grace of manner or definiteness of insight or whatever, does not proceed from will but from natural interest. Still, no one is free, not even Nick, from the will to control the future, and awkwardness is therefore an inevitable attribute of being alive. Nick only hopes that it can be minimized.

The series of novels alternates between the slow-motion scenes at which Powell excels and more static portraits of eccentrics, at which he is more mechanical. Still, these eccentrics set the outer limits of his moral world; they stand as permanent markers of experience and as warning posts. They are eccentric primarily because they lack the talent for slow-motion living. Either they cannot take a sustained interest in the opportunities and demands of the present, or they want to bolt through the present to the future. Powell subtly inflects both incapacities.

Each volume begins with its presiding eccentric—Uncle Giles in *A Question of Upbringing* and *The Acceptance World,* Mr. Deacon in *A Buyer's Market,* and General Conyers in *At Lady Molly's.* All are somehow in the backwash of life. Uncle Giles is a roving spirit of resentment, passive or barely occupied, angry at imagined cheatings on his inheritance, yet incapable of even planning for things to go better. He appears at moments when Nick feels depressed or is about to—at school, at dawn after the two long parties, at a run-down hotel with a woman fortuneteller at a time when Nick is especially uncertain about his future. At his best, in this tableau, he appears with the fortuneteller as the man of the past listening half hopefully to the woman in league with change and the future. But his misanthropy provides Nick at times of excitement "an exceptional expedient for preserving a sense of proportion."

Mr. Deacon has found the artist's backwash. A good Bohemian, but bad painter, he is out of fashion without ever having been in fashion. When Nick, who in childhood has known him as a fairly respectable family friend, finds him dedicating his old age to an antique shoppe and pacifist pamphlets, he feels shock as he never feels it with Uncle Giles. The older members of our families have an obligation to become passé; the older representatives of fields we are entering ought not to. By contrast, General Conyers is less eccentric, more thoughtful, but plays the viola loudly for consolation about his semi-retirement. The more daunting static character of the later novels, Tolland, who is related to almost everyone of importance in the novel, lives as a shadow following more active people, clinging to a mythical old-school tie and every relative—a grotesque forecast of Nick's possible future.

Nick's half-sympathy with all these resisters of contemporary reality is the other side, and the threatening one, of his personality. They represent the charm of giving up the process of understanding in favor of some simple solution—contempt for humanity, saving the world by pamphlets, clinging to ties that no one else recognizes, and so on. They are the lovable tempters to the life of delusion, geniuses of category; but they are also the last-ditch resisters to the life of the will. Hence Nick's permanently ambivalent attitude toward them.

The hyperactive, less lovable eccentric who wants to bolt through to the future is an established older novelist, St. John Clarke. Ironically, since he speaks only once, he makes better reading. Though Nick disclaims connection with the world of power, he shows persistent concern with dominance in human relationships. The efforts of several younger writers to control St. John Clarke produce an equivocal situation. The psychoanalytic poet and critic, clearly a man of style, dominates him— apparently—for a while; then the Marxist critic, clearly an awkward, gets control and ousts the poet. To these young writers St. John Clarke appears to be the novelist's awkward man, hopelessly out of date and boring, but presently they discover that he has controlled all the situations—has used the young intellectuals to bring himself up to date and replaced them as literary fashions changed. As he shifts from Freud to Marx to Trotsky he becomes the elder statesman of all the new movements, the touchstone of fashion, a parody, in fact, of Nick's prime virtue of flexibility. He is the dynamic, nonresident eccentric of *The Acceptance World*.

The title of this third novel has several connotations. Simply, it is a metaphor based on Widmerpool's new activity in discounting cargoes for future delivery—with several risks. Here is

> a world in which the essential element—happiness, for example— is drawn, as it were, from an engagement to meet a bill. Sometimes the goods are delivered, even a small profit made; sometimes the goods are not delivered, and disaster follows; sometimes the goods are delivered, but the value of the currency has changed.

All the characters have by now made "an engagement to meet a bill." The delivery date arrives, and the characters accept the fulfillment of their earlier promise—successful or disastrous—but only hindsight shows what the real promise was. Nick meanwhile begins to readjust his categories and substitutes his own for the preformed ones destroyed in *A Buyer's Market*. Slowly he comes to accept a basic humanity common to both the man of power and the man of imagination. (A similar intuition runs through the novels of Henry Green, but in Green the perception is cheerful, almost offhand, a natural gift.) Nick cannot arrive by intuition at a view so foreign to the question of upbringing; he can only work it out by slide rule and square. When Nick does see that some basic humanity exists, he reverses the idea of the common man, and decides that there is no "ordinary" world. "All human beings, drawn as they are at different speeds by the same Furies, are at close range equally extraordinary."

A Buyer's Market centers around acceptance and rejection in social groups. *The Acceptance World* abandons this formulation of the problem and turns to personal relations—especially the seemingly arbitrary acceptances and rejections of love. The novel tells two counterpointed love stories—Nick's affair with the sister of his school friend Peter Templer, and Peter's loss of his wife to the Marxist critic. Nick's affair develops favorably as the wife draws away from Peter. Since earlier miracles like the smart-set party have now become commonplace—the Greek hostess has lost her mystery and become a Trotskyite—the problem of happiness shifts from finding the right group to finding the right person. But what seems right in the world of the affections does not work. Peter Templer is a rich businessman and a successful ladies' man, and, when his wife forfeits the obvious advantages of her marriage, her action makes no sense: to Nick a former artist's model ought to prefer Peter Templer to any kind of critic, especially an unemployed one. Nick can only conclude that she has regressed.

He does not see his own affair as the other side of the coin. Jean Templer, who is estranged from her businessman husband, believes that she prefers an imaginative man. The affair promises the stability of a second and wiser choice, but founders on an apparent irrelevance. When she reveals that she has had an affair with a businessman whom Nick has been joking about as "not intelligent," the alliance he has visualized no longer exists for him. Finding that she has been capable, even in the past, of loving his opposite destroys his sense of the union and sets him to questioning the possibility of happiness through the perfect person:

> The card [Jean] sent was of French origin, in colour, showing a man and a woman seated literally on top of each other in an armchair upholstered with crimson plush. These two exchanged ardent glances. They were evidently on the best of terms. . . .
>
> Even allowing a fairly limited concession to its character as a kind of folk perception—an eternal girl sitting on an eternal young man's knee—the fact remained that an infinity of relevant material had been deliberately omitted from this vignette of love in action. These two supposedly good-looking persons were, in effect, going through the motions of love in such a manner as to convince others, perhaps less well equipped for the struggle than themselves, that they, too, the spectators, could be easily identified with some comparable tableau. They, too, could sit embracing in crimson chairs. Although hard to define with precision the exact point at which a breach of honesty had occurred, there could be no doubt that this performance included an element of the confidence trick.

For Nick, the mind attaches itself to ideal representations and without them would have no direction, but reality, like the future, will make no contract with these representations.

Though the main structure of the novel deals with reversals in love, the most brilliant writing concerns another clash of promise and fact. Stringham, the school ironist, has become an alcoholic. The apparent change merely carries out the unperceived logic of his youth. He remains the prankish schoolboy unable to accept adulthood—almost, as Nick says of another character, "preaching the gospel of pleasure to a congregation that has lost interest." After an "old boys'" dinner for the housemaster, Nick and Widmerpool try to get Stringham to bed, and, when he will not go, Widmerpool forces him to.

> "Great pity for a man to drink like that," said Widmerpool.
>
> I did not answer, largely because I was thinking of other matters; chiefly of how strange a thing it was that I myself should have been engaged in a physical conflict designed to restrict Stringham's movements: a conflict in which the moving spirit had been Widmerpool. That suggested a whole social upheaval: a positively

cosmic change in life's system. Widmerpool, once so derided by all of us, had become in some mysterious manner a person of authority. Now, in a sense, it was he who derided us; or at least his disapproval had become something far more powerful than the merely defensive weapon it had once seemed.

Many characters in *The Acceptance World* search for "happiness" or, failing that, take self-destructive courses like Stringham's, but Widmerpool wants dominion, not happiness, and Nick comes squarely against the fact that, in extreme circumstances, Widmerpool's way is far more adequate than his own. The bright boy still wins out in talk—

> "Look here," said Stringham, "I must be allowed to get in and out of my own bed. That is a fundamental human right. Other people's beds may be another matter. In them, another party is concerned. But ingress and egress of one's own bed is unassailable."
>
> "Much better stay where you are," said Widmerpool, in a voice intended to be soothing.

Much better he should. But a pity.

At Lady Molly's represents a turn made clearer by the fifth novel, *Casanova's Chinese Restaurant*. In these two, experiment comes to an end—and Powell's problem of maintaining interest increases. The easy-going people who congregate at Lady Molly's create a "slack" atmosphere; Nick sees all around him evidence that, as he had suspected, life is not a hoop to be leaped through. Lady Molly is respectable, but disorganized; at her house no one has to measure up to a code or a style because diversity is the aim. And throughout the novel the hitherto successful men meet reversals. The Marxist critic, Quiggin, falls from St. John Clarke's favor and trails off following an eccentric but economical earl. Widmerpool is unable to will sexual performance with a gay divorcée. If Nick's slow methods do not get him all he wants, other methods do not consistently produce success or happiness either. The interesting thing about Quiggin and Widmerpool is not their failures, though, so much as their honesty and even humanity.

The anxious confidence man like Gumbril, Jr., Adam Sykes, Raunce, and Lucky Jim does not appear in Powell at all. The nearest approach is the anxious but honest confidence man who tries to use and impress other people, but retains—even is handicapped by—a core of integrity. Quiggin, Widmerpool, and Members all try to manipulate older people who have power, but they are all men of conviction committed to ideas and temperaments too inflexible for best results. Quiggin is a convinced Marxist who will not move on to being a Trotskyite, Members does believe in psychoanalysis and asceticism, Widmerpool does believe in friendship, the old-school tie, mother, and efficiency.

This honesty fits in with the conception of the past in the long novel. What the past hands down is wrong at many points, but the prejudices it engrains become the core of the adult. Nick is the most conservative of all about meaning. He finds interest first in people who have some connection with family, school, and early life in London. He falls in love with a school friend's sister, first sees the world under the guidance of a school friend and an old family friend, marries a girl introduced to him by a university acquaintance. He finds his representative resisters to change in his family or their friends. He takes an interest in people primarily when they are connected from the past, though his interest can extend to cousins and in-laws. For him the changing world ought always to retain some appearance of the familiar. In the tight circles of the novel he is not alone. Yet he is doomed to understanding because, for the imaginative man moving toward middle age, his early world gives no sure guidance.

Casanova's Chinese Restaurant reemphasizes the mixture in living, but moves from drifting to the almost-too-tight world of marriage. By now Nick has made his preference for style-and-imagination a way of life. But suddenly the hyphens disappear with a return to one problem of *A Buyer's Market:* style may not be the same thing as imagination, however joined they are in one person. The two parallel marriages which provide the overt conflict reflect obliquely again Nick's own problem. A composer marries an actress, who understands career thoroughly and music partly. A music critic has been married for eight or nine years to a woman who understands neither. The marriage of the two careerists survives unsteadily; the more conventional marriage ends in the critic's suicide.

The three milieus from *A Buyer's Market* return: musicians, painters, and writers among themselves; the upper class, correctly tolerating the eccentricities of its members; and the mixed group, artists and their upper-class sympathizers. Nick, by marrying into the Tolland family, has plumped for the stability and continuity it represents for him. He has married within his own class, but not, apparently, within his interests. The family embodies the style and categories he had learned in youth, but its members lack the liveliness of the musicians and feel somewhat like adolescents with their stepmother. (Powell's upper-class world involves strong-minded women who keep high society going; ineffective but shrewd husbands; and siblings neither too jealous nor too affectionate.)

The contrast between the circles dramatizes more openly than before Nick's two sides: his identifying correctness, understatement (even to furniture and wine) with home and stability; and his taste for excitement through imaginative participation in the lives of people for whom correctness is less than all. Moreland, the composer, provides a freedom for speculation and talk that must be suppressed in the family. (Some readers complain that he seldom talks like a composer. Actually, he does talk about music, but so technically that Nick takes little interest and merely summarizes.) Nick finds him interesting as another enlisted man moving up in the ranks of the arts and meeting the problems of career and marriage in the double world of artist and aristocrat. *Casanova's Chinese Restaurant* does not have the big scenes that rise from the casual ones in the earlier novels; it excels in sudden confrontings and unpredictable relations. Stringham's mother, a domineering woman who has completely subdued her husband, an ex-naval officer, becomes the captive of the dandified actor Norman Chandler. Stringham himself, the man with the brilliance but not the discipline for the arts, again carries the pathos—and the threat—of the comedy. He snake-charms the critic's wife, who hates music and her husband, but once again bows to a caretaker, this time his mother's former secretary.

> 'But I haven't agreed to come with you yet,' said Mrs Maclintick, with some archness. 'Don't be too sure of that.'

'I recognize, Madam, I can have no guarantee of such an honour,' said Stringham, momentarily returning to his former tone. 'I was not so presumptuous as to take your company for granted. It may even be that I shall venture forth into the night—by no means for the first time in my chequered career—on a lonely search for pleasure.'

'Wouldn't it really be easier to accept my offer of a lift?' said Miss Weedon.

She spoke so lightly, so indifferently, that no one could possibly have guessed that in uttering those words she was issuing an order. There was no display of power. Even Stringham must have been aware that Miss Weedon was showing a respect for his own situation that was impeccable.

'Much, much easier, Tuffy,' he said. 'But who am I to be given a life of ease?

> Not for ever by still waters
> Would we idly rest and stay . . .

I feel just like the hymn. Tonight I must take the hard road that leads to pleasure.'

'We could give this lady a lift home too, if she liked,' said Miss Weedon.

She glanced at Mrs Maclintick as if prepared to accept the conveyance of her body at whatever the cost. It was a handsome offer on Miss Weedon's part, a very handsome offer. No just person could have denied that.

'But I am not much in the mood for going home, Tuffy,' said Stringham, 'and I am not sure that Mrs Maclintick is either, in spite of her protests to the contrary. We are young. We want to see life. We feel we ought not to limit our experience to musical parties, however edifying.'

There was a short pause.

'If only I had known this, Charles,' said Miss Weedon.

She spoke sadly, almost as if she were deprecating her own powers of dominion, trying to minimise them because their very hugeness embarrassed her; like the dictator of some absolutist state who assures journalists that his most imperative decrees have to take an outwardly parliamentary form.

'If only I had known,' she said, 'I could have brought your notecase. It was lying on the table in your room.'

Stringham laughed outright.

'Correct, as usual, Tuffy,' he said.

'I happened to notice it.'

'Money,' said Stringham. 'It is always the answer.'

'But even if I had brought it, you would have been much wiser not to stay up late.'

'Even if you had brought it, Tuffy,' said Stringham, 'the situation would remain unaltered, because there is no money in it.'

Though none of the episodes develop far, *Casanova's Chinese Restaurant* is Powell's version of loving. But his focus is sharper and his depiction of love narrower than Green's. Instead of pansexual cheer and sensuous teasing, Powell shows loving as a series of power relations. Mrs. Maclintick's power over her husband, so long as she can keep him at home, comes from her invective. Matilda's competence pleases and annoys Moreland until he gains a power of frightening her through his affair with Priscilla Tolland. Mrs. Fox, her husband, and her actor add a dimension among the minor characters. Stringham charms Mrs. Maclintick by a simple offhand assumption of power to do so. If this narrowness is a limitation in portraying love, Powell at least confines himself to the aspect which he can deal with effectively. (Ironically, power is the same force for which Nick has already shown so much distaste—and so much fascination.)

The later novels also make clearer what has already emerged in the series—that imaginative participation means more for Powell than flexibility in orienting to society. The imagination is a power in its own right for enlivening and enriching experience; it seizes on meaningful actions, plays with them, slows them down to savor every aspect, enlarges them by connecting the immediate with the significant past. The imaginative man has a resource closed to the men of power, who must win to enjoy.

But, just as style and imagination, though often allied, are not the same thing, not all who fly the flag on Imagination Day are commemorating the same romanticism. Of the modern comic novelists, Cary comes nearest to the conventional understanding. For Gulley, imagination transforms ugly walls to beauty, and transforms social reality into either a reflection of himself or a rough and ready, classifiable antagonist. Bloom, in *Ulysses*, transmutes his miseries into imaginative satisfactions, though he takes in a larger part of the world around him in terms of his main obsessions. For both Joyce and Cary, imagination makes miseries worth living through. But for Nick, and presumably Powell, imagination has no such power. It is rather an instrument for knowing what actually moves people in an age lacking a clear consensus. As such it works toward consolation by universalizing the individual predicament as well as by reducing the force of inherited formulae which do not really apply. Imagination in this sense is an imprecise instrument—Nick characteristically offers several possible explanations of what is happening—but nothing like so imprecise as the "normal" tags and labels.

In other words, *The Music of Time* takes its importance now—and even its length—from its research into a tentative reconstruction of values. Its myths, if they can be called that, represent social reality rather than supernatural, and so can be tested by imagination working on social life. This empirical mode denies that human values lie in anything that can be formulated as a large abstraction. They lie in the actual choices which people see as possible and in the actions, feelings, and results which follow. Powell does not deny the power of abstractions—social justice, for example—to move many people, but he finds a comic contradiction between what they say moves them and how they act. In the later novels of the series, this understanding of complexity in human nature and its situations becomes not merely a means of orienting the self in the world, but a value in itself. For Powell shows that, however naturally equipped, well oriented, or flexible a man may be, a residue of defeats and unwanted compromises remains inevitable. Knowing how these occur, and must occur, at once enlarges the soul and reduces angry confusion.

But, reduced to the simplest terms, what does all this imagination work upon? Upon the values of two generations Powell has lived through—one which saw man defining himself through freedom and the pleasure principle and a later one which sees the defining in planned, presumably central activity. In minia-

ture, the elegy for Stringham and Widmerpool's mysterious enthusiasm for work become the poles of the novel—discovered by
a man who understands Stringham and reports Widmerpool as
fact and, of course, portent. If there is a conciliatory middle—
and there may not be—it belongs to Nick, the narrator.

CHAPTER TEN

A Summary History

THE DEVELOPMENT OF a sub-genre like the comic novel differs from that of the novels themselves. What the critic has chosen for analysis and what he thinks about stream or process will control what he sees as development. Moreover, literature works through strong individualities rather than massed votes, and the diversities discussed have been numerous. Throughout, however, my assumption has been that a live tradition operates as a progressing conversation around some central themes. In the comic novel the conversation has obviously been disorderly. Some speakers have spoken loudly, many have broken in while another had the floor, and three at least have broken off in the middle of a sentence. (Forster's confession that the times had become incomprehensible to him perhaps applies to Huxley and Waugh as well.) Like all such great disorders, however, the comic conversation can appear—from sufficient distance—as an order, which develops not so much through negations as through speakers saying to their predecessors, "You've got something there, but here is what you've left out."

But first a word about one more common denominator. As a group these comic novels recognize the unvoiced, "disrespectable" hopes of a decade or a generation and subject them to some reality principle—but without necessarily negating the hope. Comedy does trim the cloth of aspiration to the human shape, but it also identifies the aspiration. Our century of sudden enthusiasms and quick collapses has provided exceptional raw material for these processes, though individual hopes and losses are of course proceeding at any time. The comic novels characteristically move in a cycle of destroying the outworn hope, recognizing and finding symbols for the new, and testing its adequacy. (Modern comedy is not alone in doing these things.)

Destroying the old, often by satire, has been the easiest step, for the old has usually destroyed itself by loss of faith and seeks to preserve its shell by rigid forms. (Witness the ease with which Forster gets rid of suburban manners and morals in *A Room with a View*.) Satire rids itself with equal ease of the new that does not really inspire confidence—advertising or sovietization in *Antic Hay*, inflexible organization in *Concluding*. The hard task for comedy is finding scenes and actions that will express the new interest and give scope for testing it.

Since this new hope must have some basis in society, it is not really new. It grows out of the past and has been there all the time—obscured by the overemphasis on something else. The believers in the next convolution may have been inarticulate or merely embarrassed at being unfashionable. At one important turning point, for example, Henry Green recognized the defeat of the party-going hopes and located a new area of play in the factory workers of *Living* and the servants of *Loving*. He tested the possibility of enjoyment in a milieu of organized, productive work. Readers were waiting for him without knowing it. The aristocratic scene of Huxley and Waugh, like the subjective scene of Joyce, tried to remove play as far as possible from outside interference. Readers as a group could not test these full-time pleasure ideals; they must by necessity test them within just such a world as Green's. If Green was right about workers in the middle thirties, as he was certainly unorthodox in the age of the proletarian novel, the workers had known that much for years. The intellectuals had not perceived the possibility because they preferred the all-or-nothing gamble in Huxley and Waugh. So Green had to wait for a situation that would enforce the necessity of organized work—the war—to gain a hearing.

For all its facing of limitations, this comedy has not simply enforced prudence. As Forster says in *Howard's End*, proportion, if it is not to be pedantic, must come in as a last resort. (Ordinary obsessiveness usually insures that it does.) The modern comic novel recognizes mistakes, but also the new turns people are about to take or have taken, and the limits they have met or are about to meet. This kind of comedy has its sources in pain, but it also sifts out what is left after the tragic possibilities have been given their due. It makes disillusion as well as hope compromise with the actual.

With this much prelude, we can now look at the conversation around some central themes. Obviously, the comic novel has participated in a continuing adjudication between past and present. Though Forster appears here as a fixed point, actually his comedy too is in motion; but the motion is evolutionary. Margaret's ideal of imaginative self-management is an ideal of orderly change, and Howard's End itself—the house—stands for this progression from generation to generation. Margaret cannot be Mrs. Wilcox, but she is enough like her to be her heir. Presumably the child romping in "such a crop of hay as never" will be like neither Margaret nor Helen nor Leonard, but will combine some of Margaret's control, Helen's sympathy, and Leonard's honesty. Forster sees a desirable change in manners and mores as already under way and destined to prevail. The natural man, George Emerson or Leonard Bast, is beginning to modify the best elements in the overcivilized society and will modify them more in the next generation. (*A Passage to India,* published after the war, shows no such confidence.)

The threats to this progression are anger, misunderstanding, and hence isolation, but Forster wants community and foresees it for those of similar backgrounds and tastes after the unfit have dropped away or been absorbed. He writes a comedy of the established joke—Margaret and Helen remembering Tibby's spilling coffee, Helen practicing her speech and making jokes over Leonard's head. In this community the characters receive inspiration from the mother, avoid coercion from the father, and establish a bond through sympathetic intelligence.

This evolutionary spirit died with the war. The postwar novelists do not want that kind of continuity, and do not want community on the terms available. Joyce not only feels individual separateness more than the possibility of communion; he likes it better. A mysterious community exists all around his isolated heroes. "The others"—Simon Daedalus, the barmaids—

achieve it effortlessly. The clichés Joyce satirizes so ruthlessly create a camaraderie that the more sensitive Bloom cannot join, just as Stephen cannot join the politico-literary group in the library and must play his solo about *Hamlet*. Joyce's major heroes do not become isolated; like Lenehan and the bank clerk in *Dubliners,* they choose isolation, and then suffer regrets over their loss.

Joyce and Huxley write about one of comedy's "natural" subjects, play. (The presumed Dionysian origins of comedy make a useful metaphor for naturalness.) Joyce and Huxley also had the advantage of writing in a period which tried to erect play into a major moral principle. Huxley's characters act out their programs, Joyce's more passive characters develop them inwardly, but the motives are similar. One continuing comedy in *Ulysses* proceeds from Bloom's ability to extemporize on possibilities that he has no intention of acting on. His vision of a loaf of bread, a jug of wine, and thou beside me in an olive grove gives him enough satisfaction. His post office game with Martha Clifford affords pleasure without risk. His *voyeurism* with Gertie is erotic play without chance of rejection. His financial failures become speculations on how the tavern keeper got his start or how a dignitary's hat fits. This inner-directed comedy helps give Bloom his resilience; its epitome comes in questions like "Where does tap water come from?"

As Stanley Poss has said, *Ulysses* is a comedy of stasis, with no real meeting of minds.* The Telemachus-Ulysses relation has less tension than many critics find simply because Bloom expects so little from the outer world and takes so much pleasure in private games. (The language play of *Finnegan's Wake* is a logical outcome of this preference.) The melodramatic actions that Harry Levin cites as efforts to give the novel action do not, however, test the essential Bloom. Everything stops him in real life, but nothing stops his games. Joyce is thus the most programmatic of modern comic novelists. He never brings the subterranean ideal that the novel recognizes up against its inner limitations. The limitations shown are external—Molly, Stephen, the Citizen—and prove only that imaginative play cannot

* Stanley Horn Poss, "Joyce: The Immobilized Act," Ph.D. dissertation, University of Washington, 1959.

control the environment. Even the hallucination scene which, by its nature and place in the novel, should test the ideal ends cheerfully: Bloom gets masochistic satisfaction from his humiliations and seems unshaken. The odd flatness of *Ulysses*—the sense of few emotional ups and downs—results from its presenting a program of play without bringing it into collision with anything internally threatening. *Ulysses,* though unquestionably a great novel, is a celebration rather than a test. In spite of some nostalgia, Bloom has cut his losses so much that he has obscured them.

Antic Hay, which comes into the conversation almost simultaneously with *Ulysses,* also accepts separateness as a fact, but suggests that a more active spirit may create some kind of self partly able to control the environment. Huxley sees that several traditional ideals—romantic expansiveness, neoclassic poise, the lady and the lady-killer—retain some force, even without much social support. If the present seems amiably weak in meaningful programs, the novel asks, can we not skip back over the fathers to the grandfathers and beyond? Each man can select his self and mold it on a model from the past. No one has any trouble selecting his myth, but few can live their roles. Lypiatt cannot be Michelangelo, Shearwater cannot duplicate the revolutionary discoveries of Victorian science, Rosie cannot be a great lady, and Gumbril is less than a Complete Man.

But the characters have partly protected themselves against this difficulty by forming their loose coterie. Within it each gains some recognition for his chosen role—but only some, for the chief order of entertainment is pecking away at others' vulnerable hopes. Still, even Coleman, who sees himself as a satanist sent to destroy these doubtful programs, accepts at least their relevance. He might turn his destructive talents in any direction—against Tories, for example. His choice of the avant-gardists accepts their thinly guarded faiths as important. Huxley's coterie follows the logic of Forster's, excluding the unfit, but tries to create a family from a group with similar concerns. These people trying to build lives from myths need others to recognize their inventions as real or, even in destroying them, to treat them as worth destroying and therefore having some force.

Waugh transforms Huxley's myths into fashions in rebellion.

What in Huxley had to be experimented with and discovered becomes in Waugh prescriptive. The prescriptions are simple enough for anyone to learn: communion is here for the asking, there's nobody to stop you; join any group, so long as it's new and fashionable. Where Joyce shows play of mind as enjoyable, Waugh shows play in action as a moral imperative. You must have fun or be the village idiot, the culture tells his characters. It's what your psyche needs. But, the prescription fails to add, does the psyche need the exhibitionism and anxiety that go along with this program? For the best equipped, there are obstacles to making the pleasure principle a fashion, and many people cannot play the game at all.

But Huxley, Joyce, and Waugh operate on a letter of credit from the past. It is real enough, even haunting enough, to make the exposure of its weaknesses an important need. When exposure and destruction become complete, as they do with Waugh, this kind of comedy reaches its end, turns back on itself, and admits a nostalgia for the destroyed inheritance. Waugh's honesty in *A Handful of Dust* lies in seeing that, though pleasure as a style in destruction impales itself, the past cannot be rebuilt.

Huxley and Waugh end in an awareness that some dearly held aims are impossible—for them, awareness is finally all. Green's genius is for seeing how life can be lived with such awareness. He recognizes that the particular anguish Huxley and Waugh find comes from the *unlimitedness* of their ideals. In the logic of their work this anguish is inevitable and will interfere with any effort to make ambition, pleasure, or style into moral imperatives. Green accepts this recognition briskly, but he also shows people in considerable pain finding some pleasure. His characters recognize their situation, limit their aims, live with the anxiety of being human, and enjoy the satisfactions possible in a short-run world.

Green locates the center of pain, not in the way of the world, but in the individual's magnifying his fears or wishes while all but ignoring the possible. *Concluding* tests the chances of enjoyment in an environment where coercion is at its maximum and on a day when the threat of disaster looms largest, yet finds that Mr. Rock has had a good day. Even Miss Edge has done what she set out to do, give a party, though she fails when she proposes marriage to Mr. Rock. Green is a revolutionary in changing the form of the question from pleasure or pain to pleasure-and-pain—in more extreme terms, joy-with-anguish.

In *Caught,* which is not a comic novel, and *Back,* which is, Green faces directly the dead end to which Waugh's awareness leads—nostalgia for the destroyed past. Richard Roe, in *Caught,* believes that his life went wrong somewhere about the time his son was kidnaped, even though no harm happened to the boy. He romanticizes this past until the present becomes all but unbearable. He sees in Pye, the promoted fireman, a lesson in how obsession with the past as guilt leads to suicide, but Roe cannot work through to a positive direction. He can, however, meet the crisis of fire-fighting in London and thus partly down his memories.

Back also begins where *A Handful of Dust* leaves off, in a grotesque comedy of angry confusion. Charley Summers returns from the war to visit a rose-entwined cemetery, where Rose, his adulterous love of the old days, lies buried. In a prison camp he has so built up the fantasy of her perfection that he can think of nothing else. He even encourages his landlady to talk about war-time prices so as to hear over and over the word "rose." But Green insists—by allowing the reader to make up his own mind about Rose—that the nostalgia is a disease produced by anger at the present and future. Yet even during this phase Charley takes a stoic satisfaction in organizing his work as a production manager. When he meets Nancy, Rose's half sister, and insists on recognizing her as Rose, Nancy will have none of this, and her vitality makes his recovery possible. In Green the person looking for human interest can find it if he will only recognize it; the hazard lies in denying its existence. Charley wavers between recognition and denial, but finally wins through to a hopeful future with Nancy, who is maternal and loving where Rose was willful and self-centered. Yet he does not, cannot, recover from the disease; his partial recovery gives him partial ability to live in the present and future. The novel ends:

> Then he knelt by the bed, having under his eyes the great, the overwhelming sight of the woman he loved, for the first time with-

out her clothes. And because the lamp was lit, the pink shade seemed to spill a light of roses over her in all their summer colours, her hands that lay along her legs were red, her stomach gold, her breasts the colour of cream roses, and her neck white roses for the bride. She had shut her eyes to let him have his fill, but it was too much, for he burst into tears again, he buried his face in her side just below the ribs, and bawled like a child.

"Rose," he called out, not knowing he did so, "Rose."

"There," Nancy said, "there," pressed his head with her hands. His tears wetted her. That salt water ran down between her legs. And she knew what she had taken on. It was no more or less, really, than she had expected.

This capacity for engaging the battle at its crucial points and giving life to tentative solutions does much to make Green the best British novelist since Joyce. No one else has shown comparable skill and range.

Yet pleasure-and-pain, recovery-with-disease, will not satisfy everybody. If pain is strong and omnipresent enough, a demand for pure joy as the only compensation worth having can arise. Joyce Cary at his best assumes pain so strong and omnipresent as to be barely worth describing, and pushes toward the good feeling "without the help of anyone on earth." His echoes of Joyce are honest ones, for he picks up play of mind and transforms it to creative play—hence moral rather than merely pleasurable. Cary in his best work wants complete transcendence: out of Gulley's destructive anger must come an ecstatic affirmation. (The hope is a little like the transcendence in *Wuthering Heights*—perfect hate transformed into perfect love.) By subjecting this ideal to ridiculous scenes and to the hero's own ridicule of himself and the world, Cary comes nearer than any comic contemporary to making the miracle of ecstasy out of pain ring true. Yet the balance is so precarious, so likely to become demonstration, that Cary is able to sustain the action in only one complete novel. His other novels have flashes of "a fearful joy" followed by quantities of demonstration.

But, again, Gulley's canny, reckless pursuit of creative ecstasy is not for everybody. The postwar period produced its own rage for order. People determined to set up their own security and continuity may find Gulley only a holiday companion. The two best comic novelists since the war recognize this dislocation and ask what meaningful excitements can exist within it. They ask whether people can stand that much security and whether, in fact, security as a set of habits can even exist for long.

Hartley's *Eustace and Hilda* traces in detail a developing neurotic pattern—Eustace's childhood dependence on his older sister—and its collision with adult realities. The novel makes the greatest use of psychoanalytic patterns in the genre so far, and follows exactly the psychoanalytic logic: the pattern will repeat itself indefinitely unless the individual somehow recognizes its causes. Hartley's adult novels, however, assume a security based on familiar circumstances and people. The characters' suppressed wish for less constricted lives threatens the carefully built stability, and the attempt to break out that follows leads to panic. The character cannot control the new situation and finally retreats searching for peace of mind.

Both Hartley and Powell exploit one side of Green's legacy—the neurotic burden. Their heroes want the fresh and exciting life, but they come to it handicapped by the "question of upbringing." Green all but ignores personal history to concentrate on inherited social patterns. Powell and Hartley turn the conversation by emphasizing the age's accumulated knowledge of personality as repeated experience. For Hartley these habits become so inhibiting as to threaten disintegration. Powell takes up the possibility that understanding the repeated experience may make the shocks of life more bearable. Though he returns to the party-going scene of the twenties and thirties, he sees it in this perspective of the fifties. Like Green, he values the social inheritance—so much, in fact, that he projects the personal problem itself on to the social scene. Nick's story of his own life appears through the life history of the society. He defines himself within a group also defining itself, and by his likes and dislikes establishes his own sense of identity and reality. His habitual patterns break down a little at a time, re-form to include the new self-knowledge, break again before the unexpected, and again re-form. By contrast, Hartley's characters suppress their shock at the new until outbreak occurs, but both Powell and

Hartley see more sharply than Huxley and Waugh that every step toward renewal of interest brings a conflict with "the conservative dark."

In Green's *Nothing*, John Pomfret and Mrs. Weatherby, survivors from the fun-seeking generation, puzzle over their "dull" children's interest in their civil service jobs. The best novels of Amis, Wain, and Braine derive their comedy from this new game of career. The newest generation's work has unquestionably damaged the concept of the gentleman, which has created a major difference between British and American comedy. Powell and Hartley do not take the gentleman as an effective ideal, but his presence gives their novels a basis of contrast. Hartley, for example, sets his form of play (rowing) in opposition to the status concept represented by the retired military men. Powell puts the values of the leisure class, which assumes its rights in the world, against the career drive of artists and businessmen. The aristocratic sense that men define themselves by what they do when they are freest to choose is a dimension missing from the younger men's work.

The younger novelists show the rebellion against opportunity. The remnants of the gentlemanly tradition means to their heroes only status, not value. Lucky Jim's professor has the power and position that the "ordinary chaps" would like to have, but, once in office, they would never continue the musical soireés. Braine's Joe wants the cars, clothes, and girls of the leisure class, but not the leisure. Prosperity gives him the chance for power and status, but he complains of the price. In Amis, Braine, and Wain, the heroes usually try to pay the price. Even the factory and delinquent heroes of a still younger novelist, Allan Sillitoe, represent only a more extreme rebellion against the cost of success. The crucial consideration about the young men remains not class origin, but class fate: they represent the white-collar mentality, half eager to benefit from going institutions, half resistant to them.

Quantitatively, at least, the rebellion against opportunity seems to be carrying the day; but the younger novelists have had trouble going on. They have yet to face the unsatisfactory achievement that Hartley treats or the retarded progress toward an unclear goal that Powell manages so well. Whether they can go on from the first discovery of a world they never made to more mature comedy is the most interesting question visible in English fiction.

For all their differences, though, the comic novelists have another direction in common. They have attacked an issue that can be put many ways—a superego problem, a preference for existence over essence, and so on. Their agreement about rapid obsolescence of programs is a symptom. Theorists often say that comedy depends upon type characters, but these novelists have found their strongest tensions between the pre-existing type and the individual or idiosyncratic. They have had a part in the effort taking place on many fronts to reduce the power of category, type, myth over actual human possibility. From Huxley to Powell, life trying to elevate itself toward category has slowly given way to life trying to find itself more directly.

The powerful form which category took in the first quarter of the century was myth. More or less scientific anthropology provided evidence that some universal ideals could apparently survive the decline of revealed religion. Parallel myths in diverse cultures suggested basic aspirations independent of theology. Jung and the theosophists applied these findings in different, and similar, ways. Comparative religion offered some further hope for universals. Comparative literature, to which Eliot gave so much prestige, was a "scientific" attempt, too, to find ideals surviving through the "tradition," the culture of the whole past. (The quarrel of science and literature exemplified by Richards was really a civil war, literary collector against scientific collector, with the real issue the nature of proof.) Eliot's early poetry wants to unite ideal category with actual existence and in the interim to insist upon the disparity between the two. The later "still moments" make the gap appear to close.

Huxley seems almost to be answering Eliot in advance: people do respect the high plane, but they cannot live by it. Impossible hopes create only pain. Joyce, the forerunner of so much in the contemporary novel, has a foot in each camp. His Homeric story does provide a superego for the reader, and in its terms Bloom is a Lilliputian. Yet the Joyce-without-myth movement in current criticism embodies a truth. Existence does overwhelm myth in the novel: Bloom seems better than Ulysses. Forget the melodrama and the technical tricks and he remains a man trying to meet life without valid universal ideas. He contrasts with the categorical thinking that the Daedaluses, father and son, represent in low and high form. In *Ulysses* life constantly fails to meet the standards of myth, but constantly surpasses it by a superior complexity. The failure of Stephen and Bloom to get together is unimportant. Stephen is wrong; Bloom appeals past him to the reader.

Waugh shows category losing its religious emotion and turning to social hedonism, but he retains the belief in category. Green and Powell attack the concept itself. Green's conversations about writing do not emphasize the problems discussed here, but the difficulty of achieving immediacy—real people apparently present on the printed page. He tries for this kind of reality by playing up the contradictoriness rather than the typicalness of his characters. He elevates the humanness of idiosyncrasy and lowers the humanness of set standards. (Perhaps he merely expands the meaning of "type," but, if so, he does it significantly.)

Powell does something similar from the opposite side. He comes on people from their remoteness, not their immediacy. His characters appear first through a maze of category—something a little like Robert Penn Warren's Idea—and only gradually take on their own definite existences. Yet, when they do, the narrator concludes that there are no types. Seen at close range, all people are equally extraordinary. Green cuts through myth toward a devalued, understandable person; Powell works his way out dragging his feet; but both give form to a view of personality more circumstantial than Huxley's or Waugh's.

I have called the contemporary comic novelists miniaturists, exploiting limited angles of vision, because they seem so compared to the first generation's free-wheeling hopes. Yet their circumstantiality suggests that they have as many, if not more, ideas than their predecessors—and more complex ones at that. They seem smaller because they take a more limited view of the possible. The categories they recognize are activities existing in society rather than quasi-religious images of what human nature *ought* to be. The war between category and individual goes on, with the category wanted, hated, threatened, clung to, but the recent comic novelists have narrowed the gap by making the categories more seen than unseen. (The human mind being what it is, no one need fear their complete destruction.)

If R. W. B. Lewis is right in *The Picaresque Saint*, the best serious novelists of the second generation, attempting to create disguised saints, have elevated their heroes toward existing myths. By contrast, the comic novelists have recognized a similar conflict, but have tried to reduce, and thus make more human, the power of category itself.

Comedy traditionally reduces, of course, but most of my discussion has concerned its expanding. To sum up that in one distant, distorting paragraph, these novelists have asserted the claim of active and imaginative play while recognizing the threat and pain inevitable in controlling the self and the environment. In an age rich enough to make free play seem widely possible—and dangerous enough to threaten everything—they have tested whether such an ideal can evolve, adapt to older ways, be fun, be moral, compromise with emotional illness, survive wars, and make terms with individual diversity. The range of test provides the most impressive guarantee that this comedy treats the real and important.

My summary history, like my analyses of the novels, means to be suggestive rather than definitive. Nothing would please me more than to have others go further—though my pleasure would lessen if they proved me totally wrong.

A Selected Bibliography

JOYCE CARY

Adam International Review, XVIII (November–December, 1950). Issue on Cary.

Adams, Hazard. "Blake and Gulley Jimson: English Symbolists," *Critique,* III (Spring–Fall, 1959).

———. "Joyce Cary: Posthumous Volume and Criticism to Date," *Texas Studies in Literature and Language,* I (Autumn, 1959).

———. "Joyce Cary's Three Speakers," *Modern Fiction Studies,* V (Summer, 1959).

Allen, Walter. *Joyce Cary* (supplement to *British Book News*). London, 1953.

Bettman, Elizabeth R. "Joyce Cary and the Problem of Political Morality," *Antioch Review,* XVII (Summer, 1957).

Case, Edward. "The Free World of Joyce Cary," *Modern Age,* III (Spring, 1959).

Collins, Harold R. "Joyce Cary's Troublesome Africans," *Antioch Review,* XIII (Fall, 1953).

Craig, David. "Idea and Imagination: A Study of Joyce Cary," *Fox* (published by Aberdeen University Classical, Literary, and Philosophical Societies), n.d. (c. 1954).

French, Warren G. "Joyce Cary's American Rover Girl," *Texas Studies in Literature and Language,* II (Summer, 1960).

Hamilton, Kenneth. "Boon or Thorn? Joyce Cary and Samuel Beckett on Human Life," *Dalhousie Review,* XXXVIII (Winter, 1959).

Hatfield, Glenn W., Jr. "Form and Character in the Sequence Novels of Joyce Cary." Ph.D. dissertation, Ohio State University, 1956.

Hoffman, Charles G. "Joyce Cary and the Comic Mask," *Western Humanities Review,* XIII (Spring, 1959).

———. "Joyce Cary: Art and Reality: The Interaction of Form and Narrator," *University of Kansas City Review,* XXVI (Summer, 1960).

Holloway, John. "Joyce Cary's Fiction: Modernity and 'Sustaining Power,'" *Times Literary Supplement,* August 7, 1959.

Johnson, Pamela Hansford. "Three Novelists and the Drawing of Character: C. P. Snow, Joyce Cary, and Ivy Compton-Burnett," in *Essays and Studies by Members of the English Association,* N.S., III (1950).

Karl, Frederick R. "Joyce Cary: The Moralist as Novelist," *Twentieth Century Literature,* V (January, 1960).

Kerr, Elizabeth M. "Joyce Cary's Second Trilogy," *University of Toronto Quarterly,* XXIX (April, 1960).

Kettle, Arnold. *An Introduction to the English Novel,* Vol. II. London, 1953.

King, Carlyle. "Joyce Cary and the Creative Imagination," *Tamarack Review,* X (Winter, 1959).

Meriwether, James B. "The Books of Joyce Cary: A Preliminary Bibliography of English and American Editions," *Texas Studies in Literature and Language,* I (Fall, 1959).

Murry, John Middleton. "Coming to London," *London Magazine,* III (July, 1956).

Prescott, Orville. "Two Modern Masters: Cozzens, Cary," in *In My Opinion.* Indianapolis, 1952.

Ryan, Marjorie. "An Interpretation of Joyce Cary's *The Horse's Mouth,*" *Critique,* II (Spring–Summer, 1958).

Steinbrechur, George, Jr. "Joyce Cary: Master Novelist," *College English,* XVIII (May, 1957).

Woodcock, George. "Citizens of Babel: A Study of Joyce Cary," *Queens Quarterly,* LXIII (Summer, 1956).

Wright, Andrew. "Joyce Cary's Unpublished Work," *London Magazine,* V (January, 1958).

———. *Joyce Cary: A Preface to His Novels.* London, 1958.

E. M. FORSTER

Allen, Glen O. "Structure, Symbol, and Theme in E. M. Forster's *A Passage to India,*" *PMLA,* LXX (December, 1955).

Ault, Peter. "Aspects of E. M. Forster," *The Dublin Review,* XDXXXIX (October, 1946).

Austin, Don. "The Problem of Continuity in Three Novels of E. M. Forster," *Modern Fiction Studies,* VII (Autumn, 1961).

Belgion, Montgomery. "The Diabolism of E. M. Forster," *The Criterion,* XIV (October, 1934).

Brown, E. K. *Rhythm in the Novel*. Toronto, 1950.

————. "The Revival of E. M. Forster," *The Yale Review*, XXVIII (June, 1944).

Burra, Peter. "The Novels of E. M. Forster," *The Nineteenth Century and After*, CXVI (November, 1934).

Cecil, Lord David. *Poets and Story Tellers*. London, 1949.

Connolly, Cyril. *Enemies of Promise*. New York, 1948.

Crews, Frederick C. "E. M. Forster: The Limitations of Mythology," *Comparative Literature*, XII (Spring, 1960).

Dobrée, Bonamy. *The Lamp and the Lute: Studies in Six Modern Authors*. London, 1929.

Doughty, Howard N., Jr. "The Novels of E. M. Forster," *The Bookman*, LXXV (October, 1932).

Fursell, Paul, Jr. "E. M. Forster's Mrs. Moore: Some Suggestions," *Philological Quarterly*, XXXII (October, 1953).

Hale, Nancy. "A Passage to Relationships," *Antioch Review*, XX (Spring, 1960).

Hall, James. "Forster's Family Reunions," *ELH*, XXV (March, 1958).

Harvey, John. "Imagination and Moral Theme in E. M. Forster's *The Longest Journey*," *Essays in Criticism*, VI (October, 1956).

Hoare, Dorothy M. *Some Studies in the Modern Novel*. London, 1938.

Hoffman, Frederick J. "*Howard's End* and the Bogey of Progress," *Modern Fiction Studies*, VII (Autumn, 1961).

Holt, Lee Elbert. "E. M. Forster and Samuel Butler," *PMLA*, LXI (September, 1946).

Hoy, Cyrus. "Forster's Metaphysical Novel," *PMLA*, LXXV (March, 1960).

Johnson, Elaine H. "The Intelligent Mr. E. M. Forster," *Personalist*, XXXV (Winter, 1954).

Johnstone, J. K. *The Bloomsbury Group*. New York, 1954.

Kain, Richard M. "Vision and Discovery in E. M. Forster's *A Passage to India*," in *Twelve Original Essays on Great English Novels*, edited by Charles Shapiro. Detroit, 1960.

The Kenyon Critics. *E. M. Forster*. Norfolk, Conn., 1943.

Klingopulos, G. D. "E. M. Forster's Sense of History: and Cavafy," *Essays in Criticism*, VIII (April, 1958).

Leavis, F. R. *The Common Pursuit*. London, 1952.

Macaulay, Rose. *The Writings of E. M. Forster*. New York, 1938.

Macdonald, Alastair A. "Class-Consciousness in E. M. Forster," *University of Kansas City Review*, XXVII (Spring, 1961).

McConkey, James. *The Novels of E. M. Forster*. Ithaca, N. Y., 1957.

McDowall, Frederick P. W. " 'The Mild, Intellectual Light': Idea and Theme in *Howard's End*," *PMLA*, LXXIV (September, 1959).

Maclean, Hugh. "The Structure of *A Passage to India*," *University of Toronto Quarterly*, XXII (January, 1953).

Oliver, H. J. *The Art of E. M. Forster*. Melbourne, 1960.

———. "E. M. Forster: The Early Novels," *Critique*, I (Summer, 1957).

Pedersen, Glenn. "Forster's Symbolic Form," *Kenyon Review*, XXI (Spring, 1959).

Richards, I. A. "A Passage to Forster," *The Forum*, LXXVIII (December, 1927).

Swinnerton, Frank. *The Georgian Scene*. New York, 1934.

Thomson, George H. "Symbolism in E. M. Forster's Earlier Fiction," *Criticism*, III (Fall, 1961).

———. "Theme and Symbol in *Howard's End*," *Modern Fiction Studies*, VII (Autumn, 1961).

Trilling, Lionel. *E. M. Forster*. Norfolk, Conn., 1943.

Voorhees, Richard J. "The Novels of E. M. Forster," *South Atlantic Quarterly*, LIII (January, 1954).

Warner, Rex. *E. M. Forster* (supplement to *British Book News*). London, 1950.

Warren, Austin. *Rage for Order*. Chicago, 1948.

White, Gertrude M. "*A Passage to India*: Analysis and Revaluation," *PMLA*, LXVIII (September, 1953).

Wilde, Alan. "The Aesthetic View of Life: *Where Angels Fear to Tread*," *Modern Fiction Studies*, VII (Autumn, 1961).

Wilson, Angus. "A Conversation with E. M. Forster," *Encounter*, IX (November, 1957).

Zabel, Morton Dauwen. *Craft and Character in Modern Fiction*. New York, 1957.

Zwendling, Alex. "The Novels of E. M. Forster," *Twentieth Century Literature*, II (January, 1957).

Henry Green

Allen, Walter. "An Artist of the Thirties," *Folios of New Writing*, III (Spring, 1941).

———. "Henry Green," in *Penguin New Writing*, XXV (1945).

Churchill, Thomas. "*Loving*: a Comic Novel," *Critique*, IV (Spring–Summer, 1961).

Davidson, Barbara. "The World of *Loving*," *Wisconsin Studies in Contemporary Literature*, II (Winter, 1961).

Dennis, Nigel. "The Double Life of Henry Green," *Life*, August 4, 1952.

Hall, James. "The Fiction of Henry Green: Paradoxes in Pleasure-and-Pain," *Kenyon Review*, XIX (Winter, 1957).

Labor, Earle. "Henry Green's Web of Loving," *Critique*, IV (Fall–Winter, 1961).

Melchiori, Giorgio. *The Tightrope Walkers*. London, 1956.

Phelps, Robert. "The Vision of Henry Green," *Hudson Review*, V (Winter, 1953).

Reed, Henry. *The Novel Since 1939*. London, 1946.

Russell, John. *Henry Green: Nine Novels and an Unpacked Bag*. New Brunswick, N. J., 1960.

Schorer, Mark. "Introduction to Henry Green's World," *New York Times Book Review*, October 8, 1949.

———. "The Real and Unreal Worlds of Henry Green," *New York Times Book Review*, December 31, 1950.

Southern, Terry. "The Art of Fiction," *Paris Review*, V (Summer, 1958).

Stokes, Edward. "Henry Green, Dispossessed Poet," *Australian Quarterly*, XXVIII (December, 1956).

———. *The Novels of Henry Green*. London, 1959.

Toynbee, Philip. "The Novels of Henry Green," *Partisan Review*, XVI (May, 1949).

Weatherhead, A. Kingsley. "Structure and Texture in Henry Green's Latest Novels," *Accent*, XIX (Spring, 1959).

———. *A Reading of Henry Green*. Seattle, 1961.

Welty, Eudora. "Henry Green, a Novelist of the Imagination," *Texas Quarterly*, IV (1961).

L. P. HARTLEY

Melchiori, Giorgio. "The English Novelist and the American Tradition," *Sewanee Review*, LXVIII (Summer, 1960). Reprinted from *Studi Americani*, I (1955).

"The New Novelists" (symposium), *London Magazine*, V (November, 1958). Articles by Anthony Quinton, Lettice Cooper, Frank Kermode, and Maurice Cranston.

Vernier, J.-P. "La Trilogie romanesque de L. P. Hartley," *Etudes Anglaises*, XIII (Janvier–Mars, 1960).

Webster, Harvey Curtis. "The Novels of L. P. Hartley," *Critique*, IV (Spring–Summer, 1961).

ALDOUS HUXLEY

Atkins, John Alfred. *Aldous Huxley: A Literary Study*. London, 1956.

Baker, Howard. "In Praise of the Novel: The Fiction of Huxley, Steinbeck, and Others," *Southern Review,* V (Spring, 1940).

Baldanza, Frank. *"Point Counter Point: Aldous Huxley on 'The Human Fugue,' " South Atlantic Quarterly* (Spring, 1959).

Barzun, Jacques. "The Anti-Modern Essays of Aldous Huxley," *London Magazine,* IV (August, 1957).

Brooke, Jocelyn. *Aldous Huxley*. London, 1954.

Butts, Mary. *In Scrutinies II,* edited by Edgell Rickword. London, 1931.

Daiches, David. "Aldous Huxley," in *The Novel and the Modern World*. Chicago, 1939.

Dyson, A. E. "Aldous Huxley and the Two Nothings," *Critical Quarterly,* III (Winter, 1961).

Eschelbach, Claire John, and Shober, Joyce Lee. *Aldous Huxley: A Bibliography, 1916–1959.* Berkeley, 1961.

Estrich, Helen. "Jesting Pilate Tells the Answer: Aldous Huxley," *Sewanee Review,* XLVII (January, 1939).

Glicksberg, Charles I. "Aldous Huxley: Art and Mysticism," *Prairie Schooner,* XXVII (Winter, 1953).

————. "Huxley, the Experimental Novelist," *South Atlantic Quarterly,* LII (January, 1953).

Hamill, Elizabeth. *These Modern Writers*. Melbourne, 1946.

Heintz-Friedrich, Suzanne. *Aldous Huxley: Entwicklung Seiner Metaphysik*. Bern, 1949.

Henderson, Alexander. *Aldous Huxley*. London, 1935. New York, 1936.

Hoffman, Frederick. "Aldous Huxley and the Novel of Ideas," in *Forms of Modern Fiction,* edited by William Van O'Connor. Minneapolis, 1948.

Holmes, Charles M. "Aldous Huxley's Struggle with Art," *Western Humanities Review,* XV (Spring, 1961).

Karl, Frederick R. "The Play Within the Novel in *Antic Hay,*" *Renascence,* XIII (Winter, 1961).

Kessler, Martin. "Power and the Perfect State: a Study in Disillusionment as Reflected in Orwell's *Nineteen Eighty-Four* and Huxley's *Brave New World,*" *Political Science Quarterly,* LXXII (December, 1957).

King, Carlyle. "Aldous Huxley's Ways to God," *Queens Quarterly,* LXI (Spring, 1954).

Lovett, Robert. "Vanity Fair Up-to-Date," *New Republic,* December 5,

1928. Reprinted in *Literary Opinion in America,* edited by M. D. Zabel. New York, 1937. Revised edition, 1951.

O'Faolain, Sean. *The Vanishing Hero.* London, 1951.

Rolo, Charles, ed. Introduction to *The World of Aldous Huxley.* New York, 1947.

Salvan, J. L. "Le Scandale de la Multiplicité des Consciences chez Huxley, Sartre, et Simone de Beauvoir," *Symposium,* V (November, 1951).

Savage, D. X. "Aldous Huxley and the Dissociation of Personality," in *The Withered Branch.* London, 1950. Reprinted in *The Novelist as Thinker (Focus Four)*, edited by B. Rajan. London, 1947. Reprinted from *Sewanee Review,* LV (Autumn, 1947).

Schmerl, Rudolf B. "Aldous Huxley's Social Criticism," *Chicago Review,* XIII (Winter–Spring, 1959).

Slochower, Harry. *No Voice Is Wholly Lost.* New York, 1945. London, 1946.

Watts, Harold. Introduction to *Point Counter Point.* New York, 1947.

Wilson, Colin. "Existential Criticism and the Works of Aldous Huxley," *London Magazine,* V (September, 1958).

ANTHONY POWELL

Hall, James. "The Uses of Polite Surprise: Anthony Powell," *Essays in Criticism,* XII (April, 1962).

Leclaire, Lucien A. "Anthony Powell: Biographie Spirituelle d'une Génération," *Etudes Anglaises,* IX (Janvier–Mars, 1956).

Mizener, Arthur. "A Dance to the Music of Time," *Kenyon Review,* XXII (Winter, 1960).

Vinson, James. "Anthony Powell's *Music of Time,*" *Perspective,* X (Summer–Autumn, 1958).

Voorhees, Richard J. "Anthony Powell: The First Phase," *Prairie Schooner,* XXVIII (Winter, 1954).

EVELYN WAUGH

Betjeman, J. "Evelyn Waugh," in *Living Writers* (broadcast on the Third Program, 1946). London, 1947.

Dennis, Nigel. "Evelyn Waugh and the Churchillian Renaissance," *Partisan Review,* X (Summer, 1943).

De Vitis, A. A. *Roman Holiday, The Catholic Novels of Evelyn Waugh.* New York, 1956.

Dyson, A. E. "Evelyn Waugh and the Mysteriously Disappearing Hero," *Critical Quarterly*, II (Spring, 1960).

Green, Peter. "Du côté de chez Waugh," *Review of English Literature* (Leeds), II (April, 1961).

Hall, James. "The Other Post-War Rebellion: Evelyn Waugh Twenty-Five Years After," *ELH*, XXVIII (June, 1961).

Hollis, C. *Evelyn Waugh*. London, 1954.

Lapicque, F. "Le Satire dans l'oeuvre d'Evelyn Waugh," *Etudes Anglaises*, X (Juillet–Septembre, 1957).

Linklater, E. "Evelyn Waugh," in *The Art of Adventure*. London, 1947.

Macaulay, Rose. "The Best and the Worst, II—Evelyn Waugh," *Horizon*, XIV (December, 1946). Reprinted in *Writers of Today*, 2d series, ed. by D. V. Baker. London, 1948.

Marcus, Steven. "Evelyn Waugh and the Art of Entertainment," *Partisan Review*, XXIII (Summer, 1956).

McCormick, J. *Catastrophe and Imagination*. London, 1957.

Mikes, G. *Eight Humorists*. London, 1954.

O'Donnell, Donat. *Maria Cross, Imaginative Patterns in a Group of Modern Catholic Writers*. London, 1953.

O'Faolain, Sean. *The Vanishing Hero*. London, 1951.

Rolo, Charles J. "Evelyn Waugh: The Best and the Worst," *Atlantic*, CXCIV (October, 1954).

Savage, D. S. "The Innocence of Evelyn Waugh," in *The Novelist as Thinker (Focus Four)*, edited by B. Rajan. London, 1947.

Spender, Stephen. *The Creative Element*. London, 1953.

Stopp, Frederick J. *Evelyn Waugh: Portrait of an Artist*. London, 1958.

———. "Grace in Reins," *The Month*, N.S. X (August, 1953).

———. "The Circle and the Tangent," *The Month*, N.S. XII (July, 1954).

———. "End of an Illusion," *Renascence* (Winter, 1956).

———. "Apology and Explanation," *Queens Quarterly*, LXV (Spring, 1958).

Stürzl, Erwin. "Evelyn Waughs Romanwerk: Makabre Farce oder 'Menschliche Komödie'?" *Die neueren Sprachen*, VIII (1959).

Voorhees, R. J. "Evelyn Waugh Revisited," *South Atlantic Quarterly*, XLVIII (April, 1949).

———. "Evelyn Waugh's War Novels," *Queens Quarterly*, LXV (Spring, 1958).

Wasson, Richard. "*A Handful of Dust*: Critique of Victorianism," *Modern Fiction Studies*, VII (Winter, 1961–62).

Wilson, Edmund. "Never Apologize, Never Explain," *New Yorker*, March 4, 1944. Reprinted in *Classics and Commercials*. London and New York, 1951.

Index